GreenSmoothieGirl.com Readers' Favorite Healthy Recipes

55% All Raw, 85% Vegan, & 90% Gluten Free

~ Volume 1 ~

by
Robyn Openshaw

GreenSmoothieGirl.com Readers' Favorite Healthy Recipes, Volume 1

Published by Robyn Openshaw/GreenSmoothieGirl.com
Lindon, UT
2nd Printing September 2012

ISBN 978-0-9831113-8-2

Printed in the United States of America.

Disclaimer

Nothing in this book is intended to claim to diagnose, treat, cure, or prevent any disease. This book is not a substitute for primary medical care, but should be seen rather as an educational resource.

Trademarks

All trademarks mentioned are the property of their respective owners.

Contents

(R=Raw recipe, V=Vegan recipe, GF=Gluten-free recipe)

Breads

Cereals & "Dairy"

Cereals

Milks & Creams

"Cheeses"

Salsas, Sauces, & Relishes

Salsas

Sauces

Snacks

Smoothies & Other Drinks

Smoothies

Other Drinks

About the Author

Robyn Openshaw grew up the eldest of eight children, raised on a tight budget where the menu was dominated by simple plant foods: whole grains and legumes, greens, fruits and vegetables, and nuts and seeds.

She has a Web site, GreenSmoothieGirl.com, with tens of thousands of new visitors monthly, dedicated to helping people achieve high energy and vibrant health. Its mission is to teach families how to live a whole-food lifestyle (mostly plants and 60-80% raw) diet that is easy, inexpensive, and delicious—in addition to nourishing.

Robyn taught at a university and now lectures all over the U.S. She is the author of the *12 Steps to Whole Foods* course, *The Green Smoothies Diet*, and several recipe books. She is also the author of two children's books, *The Adventures of Junk Food Dude* and *Junk Food Dude's Yummy Healthy Recipes*.

She is a single mom of four competitive athletes with high-caloric needs who help develop and test her recipes. She received undergraduate and graduate degrees from BYU and the University of Utah and loves "arranging the elements" in the kitchen, reading and writing, cycling, running, skiing, and competitive tennis.

Acknowledgments

Recipe categorization: Desirée Ward

Desirée reviewed the readers' recipes to determine if they qualified as being raw, vegan, and/or gluten free. She also occasionally suggested ingredient substitutions in order to make a recipe fit into one or more of the three categories. Her Web site featuring whole-food and gluten-free cooking is www.unconventionalkitchen.com. Contact her at desiree@unconventionalkitchen.com.

Food staging & photography: Katie Dudley

Katie is a genius with food photography, which isn't an easy subject. I know tons of photographers but recruited her specifically to shoot my recipes. Contact her at katiedudley3@gmail.com.

Editing & page design: Deb Tokarewich

Deb is a language master par excellence and nonpareil, with a fine eye for detail. (I'm a former editor and know good from better from best; thus I hire only the finest.) She also loves playing with templates, fonts, graphics, and other page design stuff. Contact her at dtokarewich@yahoo.com.

Cover design: Alana Mae Jenkins

Alana Mae's cover beat 169 other designs in a contest because I fell madly in love with her creation—it's feminine and fanciful, artistic and attention grabbing. Contact her at southcoastdesigner@hotmail.com.

Introduction

Before I radically changed my diet and thereby transformed my family's health, my best and most used recipe books were the "Favorites" collections. The business school of the university where I taught, the church congregation of my childhood, my mother-in-law's church congregation, even the U.S. Congress (whose recipe book I received in Washington D.C. when I got married)…they all put together their community's best recipes.

I always figured that something others use a few times a month, which might be loved for generations in a family, is worth a try.

The problem is, when you submit your favorite recipes, you want everyone to be impressed by how the recipe tastes. In America, that means lots of refined foods: sugar, white flour, toxic salt and, oh, a nearly endless litany of fatty ingredients.

One "favorite" in my religious community is called Funeral Potatoes because we always serve it after funerals. (It may be actually contributing to more funerals.) It contains sour cream, cheddar cheese, cream of chicken soup (with monosodium glutamate), greasy hash browns, and margarine.

Three years after putting GreenSmoothieGirl.com up, I had the largest community of whole-foods enthusiasts on the Internet—and maybe in the world. Tens of thousands read my newsletter and blog and follow my 12 Steps to Whole Foods program. One day I thought to myself, why not gather the best *healthy* recipes of my readers and put the collection out there?

And that's what this is. It's the only Favorites collection that I know of that focuses on high nutrition!

I confess I've combed through the recipes and made substitutions. If you said salt, I substituted sea (unrefined) salt. If you said sugar, I changed it to raw coconut sugar or Sucanat. If you said dairy or soy milk, I replaced it with rice or almond milk. If you said flour, I said whole-grain flour. Stuff like that. If an ingredient didn't qualify as a whole food, I made my standard substitutions.

I also confess that I haven't tested all the recipes like I do when I develop my own. I've trusted my readers. So, a caveat: you'll have to trust each other.

Keep in mind that some of my readers are long-time raw foodists, so some recipes are all raw. And some readers are new to the whole-foods journey, so their recipes may not qualify under your personal nutrition standards.

You'll get a somewhat wide variety of what's considered "healthy." But these are the recipes that make you love being health minded—recipes that taste good but also nourish you.

Thank you to all my amazing readers who contributed recipes! Each recipe has an attribution line directly beneath its title. The recipes are organized alphabetically in each section according to the contributors' first names (□□□by the recipe names). Names are written same as they were submitted; occasionally a contributor's website or blog is also included. And if I "tweaked" a recipe a bit to use even more healthful ingredients, there's an additional attribution line noting that. Last but not least, there is a letter designation after a recipe name if it qualifies as being an all-raw (R), vegan (V), and/or gluten-free (GF) recipe.

There are photos of some of the recipes in a section near the middle of the book. Each is captioned with the recipe title and page number where the recipe can be found. Recipes that have photos in this section have a "[See Photos section.]" reference at the end of the recipe. (Note that these references as well as the photo captions are hot links in the PDF version of the book; clicking on them will take you directly from the recipe to its photo, and vice versa.)

I hope you find lots of new favorites for your own arsenal. That's the key to vibrant nutrition and optimal health: having a repertoire of great recipes so you look forward to your nutritious meals and snacks.

Enjoy!

~ *Robyn Openshaw*

Breads

Breads

Zucchini Bread

Thanks for the recipe, Barbara!

(Recipe was adapted by Robyn.)

3¼ C whole-wheat flour
1½ tsp. sea salt
½ tsp. ground nutmeg or allspice
2 tsp. baking soda
1½ tsp. ground cinnamon
1½ C Sucanat or coconut palm sugar
1 C coconut oil, melted
4 eggs (organic, free range), beaten
⅓ C water
1 zucchini, grated
1 yellow squash, grated
1 carrot, grated
1 ripe banana, mashed
1 tsp. lemon juice
zest of 1 lemon
optional: 1 C chopped walnuts or pecans

Preheat oven to 350°. In a large bowl, combine flour, salt, nutmeg, baking soda, cinnamon, and sugar. In a separate bowl, combine oil, eggs, water, zucchini, and lemon juice. Mix wet ingredients into dry until just combined, then fold in nuts (if using). Bake in two standard loaf pans, sprayed with nonstick spray, for 1 hour or until a tester comes out clean. Alternatively, bake in five mini loaf pans for about 45 min. *Makes 5 mini or 2 regular loaves.*

Coconut Banana Bread with Lime Glaze (GF)

Thanks for the recipe, Desirée Hancock (www.unconventionalkitchen.com)!

This is a fabulous bread to take to parties and get-togethers. I always get asked for this recipe.

2½ C whole-grain flour (kamut, oat, spelt/barley/brown rice mixture)
¾ tsp. baking soda
½ tsp. salt
1 C Sucanat
¼ C (4 Tbsp.) coconut oil, softened
2 large eggs (organic, free range)
1½ C (about 4 large) mashed ripe bananas
¼ C plain yogurt
3 Tbsp. apple juice or almond milk*
1 tsp. vanilla extract
½ C shredded coconut
2 Tbsp. additional shredded coconut (for topping)
⅓ C powdered Sucanat whisked with 2 Tbsp. fresh lime juice *OR* ¼ C agave whisked with 1½ Tbsp. fresh lime juice (for glaze)

Preheat oven to 350°. Whisk flour, baking soda, and salt together and set aside.

In a large mixing bowl, beat butter and sugar until blended. Add eggs and beat to combine. Add banana, yogurt, apple juice/milk, and vanilla. Beat until blended. Add flour mixture and beat at a low speed until just combined. Stir in ½ C coconut.

Pour batter into a 9"x5" loaf pan that has been sprayed with nonstick spray. Sprinkle additional 2 Tbsp. coconut on top.

Bake about 1 hour or until a knife or skewer inserted in center comes out clean. Check bread after about 40 min. If the top has browned and the coconut pieces are looking toasty, cover top of bread lightly with a piece of foil and continue baking until done.

When done, remove pan from oven. Let cool on a cooling rack for about 10 min., then carefully remove from pan. Whisk Sucanat and lime juice together for the glaze, then drizzle over top. Cool for another 15 min. before slicing. *Makes 1 loaf.*

Soda Bread

Thanks for the recipe, Donna!

2 C whole-wheat flour
½ tsp. sea salt
1 tsp. baking soda
1 egg (organic, free range), beaten
1 Tbsp. honey (raw)
1 C plain yogurt
optional: ⅛ tsp. cardamom *OR* 1 tsp. crushed caraway

Preheat oven to 375°. Stir dry ingredients together. Beat honey and yogurt into egg, then gradually pour into dry ingredients (the combined mixture will be dry like a yeast bread dough). Blend mixture with your hands to work all flour in. If too dry, add more yogurt. If too wet, add more flour. Knead for 5 minutes.

Shape by hand into a flat loaf and place on an oiled baking sheet. Cut two parallel slashes in dough about ½" deep (this allows the dough to rise without cracking). Bake for 25-30 min. until well browned and sounds hollow in the middle. *Makes 1 small loaf.* [See Photos section.]

Yummy Cornbread

Thanks for the recipe, Evi from Germany!

(Recipe was adapted by Robyn.)

1 C whole-wheat flour
1 C organic cornmeal
1 Tbsp. baking powder (aluminum free)
½ tsp. sea salt
2-4 Tbsp. honey (raw)
2 eggs (organic, free range)
1 C rice, oat, or coconut milk
¼ C coconut oil, melted

Preheat oven to 425°. Grease the bottom and ½" up the sides of a 9"x9"x2" baking pan, then set aside. In a medium mixing bowl, stir together the flour, cornmeal, baking powder, and salt. Make a well in the center of the dry mixture, then set aside. In another bowl, combine honey, eggs, milk, and oil. Add this mixture to the dry mixture all at once. Stir until just moistened. Spoon batter into the prepared pan. Bake for 20-25 min. or until a wooden toothpick inserted near the center comes out clean. Cool on a wire rack. This is great with vegan chili or just as a snack. [See Photos section.]

Banana Bread (V)

Thanks for the recipe, Garon!

(Recipe was adapted by Robyn.)

1¼ C whole-grain flour (wheat, Kamut, and/or oat)
7 Tbsp. Sucanat or coconut palm sugar
1½ tsp aluminum-free baking powder
½ tsp. sea salt
⅛ tsp, cinnamon
2 bananas
½ C almond milk
2 tsp. nut oil
½ tsp. vanilla

Combine all dry ingredients in a bowl. In a separate bowl, combine mashed bananas, almond milk, oil, and vanilla. Add wet ingredients to dry and stir. Pour into small, greased bread pan. Bake at 325° for 1 hour.

Whole-Wheat Pita Bread (V)

Thanks for the recipe, Janelle!

1 C warm water
1½ Tbsp. yeast
1 Tbsp. molasses
1 tsp. salt
2½ C whole-wheat flour
½ C gluten flour

Preheat oven to 450°. Add all ingredients to a bread machine and run the Dough cycle.

> ***Note:*** If you don't have a bread machine: Put first 3 ingredients in a bowl and let sit for 5 min. Then add flour with salt mixed in. Mix and knead until smooth. Cover and rise for 1 hour until double in size. Punch down dough and knead for 5-10 min.

Divide dough into six portions. On floured surface, flatten each piece to about ⅛" thick with rolling pin. Cover with towel and let rise 30 min. Warm a baking sheet in the preheating oven for 2 min., then remove and sprinkle with cornmeal. Arrange dough rounds on the prepared sheet and bake 6 min. Remove from sheet and cover with a moistened towel to soften. When cooled, slice in half and use a knife to finish opening any parts of the pita pocket that didn't fully puff up. *Makes 6 pita rounds.*

Fainá (Garbanzo Flatbread) (V,GF)

Thanks for the recipe, Linda (www.lindasgoldenyears.blogspot.com)!

2½ C garbanzo bean flour
1 tsp. salt
7 Tbsp. olive oil, divided
freshly ground black pepper and/or any herbs you like, to taste
2-2½ C water, divided
optional: 2 Tbsp. Parmesan cheese [Omit for vegan recipe.]

Preheat the oven to 450°. Whisk the garbanzo bean flour together with the salt, 3 Tbsp. of the olive oil, Parmesan cheese, and a generous amount of black pepper/herbs. Whisk in 1¾ C of the water until well mixed. Set aside for about 30 min. to let the flour absorb some of the water.

When the oven is hot, place the remaining 4 Tbsp. of olive oil in a 12" pizza pan and heat in the oven until very hot. Stir more of the water into the batter until the batter is thin enough to pour. Remove hot pizza pan from oven and pour batter into the pan. It should make a thin (about ¼") layer. Place in the oven and bake until fainá is golden and crispy (about 8-10 min.). Cut into pieces and serve.

Prep Time: 45 minutes. Cook Time: 15 minutes.

Tip: This can also be cut into crackers if cooked until crispy. You can also use a smaller pan to make thicker faína, which will need a slightly longer baking time.

Breadmaker Bread (V)

Thanks for the recipe, Nina!

Note: High-altitude version.

1½ C warm water

2 Tbsp. dough enhancer or Vital Wheat gluten

1 Tbsp. potato pearls

¼ C extra virgin olive oil

¼ C agave (raw, organic) or honey (raw) *OR* ½ C reconstituted "group buy" dates [Use agave or dates for V recipe.]

2 tsp. sea salt

2 tsp. yeast

4 C freshly ground whole-wheat flour

Mix all ingredients *except* the yeast and flour in a blender for several seconds to mix well. Pour into the bread machine pan and set for Wheat loaf. Gently scoop the wheat flour on top of wet ingredients. Make a well in the flour and sprinkle yeast on top. Close and start your bread machine and forget about it for 3½ hours—then enjoy healthful, hot bread! *Makes 1 large loaf.*

Best Banana Bread Ever

Thanks for the recipe, Sara!

4-5 overripe bananas

½ C honey (raw)

½ C melted coconut oil

2 C freshly ground whole-wheat flour

2 eggs (organic, free range)

½ tsp. baking soda

½ tsp. baking powder (aluminum-free)

½ tsp. vanilla

½ tsp. sea salt

3 Tbsp. milk (any kind)

optional: raw cocoa nibs, chocolate chips, or carob chips

Beat overripe bananas until mush. Mix together with all other ingredients and bake at 350° for about 45 minutes. Bake for less time, about 25 minutes, if you are making muffins or mini bread loaves.

Carrot Walnut Loaf

Thanks for the recipe, Shannon Miles (milesholistichealth.com)!

3½ C carrot pulp
1 C apple sauce (no sugar added)
3 C whole-grain flour
1 C grapeseed oil
1 C honey (raw)
6 egg whites (organic, free range)
1 Tbsp. vanilla
1 Tbsp. baking soda
2 Tbsp. cinnamon
1 tsp. nutmeg
1 C raw walnuts, crushed

Preheat oven to 350°. Mix up the carrot pulp with the egg whites, honey, vanilla, and grapeseed oil. Sift the flour, baking soda, cinnamon, and nutmeg together, then add it gradually to mixture. Stir until blended. Mix in the nuts.

Pour the batter into a greased loaf pan making sure to leave some room (about ¼" from the top) for expansion. Top with more walnuts. Bake for 45 min. or more, depending on oven.

Suzi's Whole-Wheat Flaxseed Bread

Thanks for the recipe, Suzi!

- 2 Tbsp. yeast
- 2 Tbsp. lecithin granules
- 1 C flax seeds, ground in blender *OR* ⅓ C flaxseed oil
- ½ C honey (raw)
- 5½ C warm water
- 8 C wheat, ground (it will make about 12 C of flour)
- ½ C vital wheat gluten
- 2 Tbsp lemon juice, *not* fresh squeezed and *must* be lukewarm
- 1½ Tbsp. sea salt
- 1 C bread flour

Preheat oven to 350°. Mix the first 5 ingredients together so they are well mixed. Add 6 C of the flour to the wet mixture and knead. Add the wheat gluten and mix well. Then add the other 6 C of flour and the final 3 ingredients. Knead well until dough starts to stick together and is not so sticky.

Oil a large bowl, place dough in it, and knead a little to make one big ball. Put bowl in a warm place, cover, and let rise until double in bulk. Punch down and divide into three bread pans. Cover and let rise about 20-40 min. Bake for 26 min. The loaves will be a light brown and sound hollow when tapped gently. *Makes 3 loaves.*

Muffins/Scones

Sugar-Free Blueberry Muffins

Thanks for the recipe, Alicia!

2 C whole-wheat flour
1 tsp. baking soda
1¼ C buttermilk
2 egg whites (organic, free range), lightly beaten
⅓ C coconut oil
½ C honey (raw)
1 C fresh blueberries

Preheat oven to 350°. Sift together flour and baking soda. In a separate bowl, whisk together buttermilk, egg whites, oil, and honey until creamy, then stir in blueberries. Pour wet into dry and fold together. Pour into muffin pan and bake 25-30 min.

Grape-Nuts Morning Muffins (V)

Thanks for the recipe, Garon!

(Recipe was adapted by Robyn.)

1¼ C whole-grain flour (wheat, Kamut, and/or oat)
1 Tbsp. baking powder (aluminum free)
1 tsp. ground cinnamon
1 tsp. unrefined salt (Real Salt or Original Crystal Himalayan Salt)
1 C Grape-Nuts cereal
1 C almond milk (original flavor)
1 ripe banana, mashed
½ C unsweetened applesauce
½ C Sucanat or coconut palm sugar
2 Tbsp. coconut oil, softened

Preheat oven to 400°. Mix flour, baking powder, cinnamon, and salt in a large bowl. Mix cereal and milk in medium bowl, let stand 3 min., then stir in banana, applesauce, sugar, and coconut oil. Add to flour mixture and stir just until moistened. Batter will be lumpy. Spoon batter into muffin pan sprayed with cooking spray. Bake for 20 min. or until golden brown. For mini muffins, bake for 12 min.

Good Morning Muffins

Thanks for the recipe, Heidi (www.franticallysimple.com)!

- 2 C whole-wheat flour (white whole wheat makes for a lighter product than red)
- 1 Tbsp. ground cinnamon
- 2 tsp. baking powder (aluminum free)
- ½ tsp. baking soda
- ½ tsp. sea salt
- 2 C grated carrots and/or zucchini
- 1 apple (peeled, cored, and chopped)
- 1 C dried cranberries
- ½ C chopped nuts (pecans are especially good)
- 1 egg (organic, free range)
- 2 egg whites (organic, free range)
- ½ C raw honey or real maple syrup
- ½ C no-sugar-added applesauce, room temperature
- ¼ C melted coconut oil
- 1 Tbsp. vanilla extract

Preheat oven to 375°. Lightly oil 18 muffin cups. (Paper liners are *not* recommended. Because there is only a small amount of fat in this recipe, the paper will stick to the muffin.) In a medium bowl, whisk together eggs, egg whites, honey, applesauce, coconut oil, and vanilla. In a large bowl, stir together flour, cinnamon, baking powder, baking soda, and salt. Stir in carrots/zucchini, apples, cranberries, and nuts. Add applesauce mixture and stir until just moistened. Spoon the batter into the prepared muffin cups, filling them about ¾ full. Bake for 15-20 min. or until the tops are golden and spring back when lightly pressed. *Makes 18 muffins.*

Flax Muffins

Thanks for the recipe, June!

1½ C oat bran
1 C brown sugar
1 C all-purpose flour
1 C buttermilk
1 C flaxs eed, ground
½ C coconut oil
1 C wheat bran
2 eggs (organic, range free)
1 Tbsp. baking powder
1 tsp. baking soda
½ tsp. sea salt
1½ C raisins
2 oranges, peeled and seeded
1½ C walnuts, chopped

Preheat oven to 375°. Coat two 12-cup muffin tins with cooking spray. In a large bowl, combine oat bran, flour, flax seed, wheat bran, baking powder, and salt. Set aside. In a blender, combine oranges, brown sugar, buttermilk, oil, eggs, and baking soda. Blend well, then pour orange mixture into dry ingredients. Add raisins and nuts and mix well. Divide into muffin tins. Bake 18 min. Cool for 5 min.

Cranberry Scones (V,GF)

Thanks for the recipe, Linda!

2 C grated carrots (about 2 carrots)
2 C grated apples (about 2 apples)
2 C walnuts
2 C raisins
1 C cranberries (fresh or frozen)
1 C flax seeds
4 Tbsp. raw agave nectar
¼ C fresh lemon juice
2 Tbsp. extra virgin olive oil
optional: 2 Tbsp. sesame seeds (hulled or unhulled)

Use the S blade in your food processor. Add the walnuts to the dry food processor bowl and grind thoroughly. Take the blade out and use a plastic spatula to pour the walnuts into a large mixing bowl.

Slice carrots into approximately 1" chunks, put them into the processor, and grind them until they are a fine consistency. Remove blade and pour the carrots into the bowl with the walnuts.

Put the S blade back into the processor and repeat same process with the apples; pour the apples into the same mixing bowl.

Add the raisins, cranberries, raw agave nectar, lemon juice and olive oil into the bowl.

In a high-powered blender or clean coffee grinder, mill the flax seeds to a powder. Add the ground flax seeds to the mixing bowl and start mixing the ingredients with both hands. Keep mixing the dough until there are no chunks or dry pockets left. You are encouraged to think happy thoughts while doing this :-)

Place a Teflex or other nonstick sheet over the plastic mesh of your dehydrator tray. Using an ice cream scoop, scoop mounds of dough onto the tray (any spoon will do, but the scoop makes it more uniform). Position the scones close together as they will shrink while drying.

For an attractive finish, sprinkle sesame seeds on top. Dehydrate at 105°-115° for approximately 15-20 hours, then flip the scones and dehydrate for another 3 hours.

The scones will keep in a glass or a plastic container for up to 2 months in the refrigerator or for 2 weeks at room temperature. *Makes 25 scones.*

Almond Muffins (GF)

Thanks for the recipe, Sharlene!

1½ C raw almonds
¼ C pure maple syrup
3 eggs (organic, free range)
1 tsp. vanilla
¼ tsp. sea salt
optional: zest of 1 lemon or orange

Preheat oven to 375°. Combine syrup, eggs, vanilla, and sea salt in a small bowl and mix well. In a blender, grind almonds until flour-like consistency. (Use a spatula to scrape the sides if the almonds become sticky.) While the blender is grinding the almonds, slowly pour in the liquid mixture. Continue to blend until it is mixed thoroughly. Oil and flour a muffin tin. Pour batter into the tin. Bake 11 min. until golden brown. *Makes about 6 standard-sized muffins.*

Tip: Feel free to experiment with different kinds of nuts. 1 C almonds, ¼ C walnuts, and ¼ C pecans is a nice combination also. Brazilian nuts are also fantastic!

Orange-Bran-Flax Muffins

Thanks for the recipe, Tammy!

(Recipe was adapted by Robyn.)

1½ C rolled oats
½ C whole-wheat (or spelt or Kamut) flour
½ C walnuts or pecans
1 C flax seeds
1 C natural wheat bran or whole-wheat flour
1 Tbsp. baking powder (aluminum free)
2 whole oranges, washed, quartered, and seeded
1 C Sucanat or coconut palm sugar
1 C buttermilk
½ C extra virgin olive oil
2 eggs (organic, free range)
1 tsp. baking soda (aluminum free)
1½ C mixed dried berries or Craisins

Preheat oven to 375°. Blend oats to a course meal in a high-speed blender. Separately blend nuts and flax seed until coarsely ground in the blender. In a large bowl, combine oats, flour, nuts and flaxseed, bran, baking powder, and salt. Set aside. In a blender or food processor, blend well the oranges, sugar, buttermilk, oil, eggs, and baking soda. Pour orange mixture into dry ingredients and mix until well blended. Stir in dried berries or Craisins. Fill paper-lined muffin tins almost to the top. Bake for 15-20 min. or until wooden toothpick inserted in center comes out clean. Cool 5 min. before removing to cooling rack.

Pumpkin Muffins (V)

Thanks for the recipe, Tish!

1 (16 oz.) can pumpkin purée (can substitute with sweet potato or butternut squash purée)
⅓ C agave (raw, organic)
⅓ C coconut oil
½ C water
1 tsp. vanilla extract
2 C whole-wheat flour
1½ tsp. baking soda
½ tsp. sea salt
optional: ½ C nuts, raisins, or carob chips

Preheat oven to 350°. Mix first five ingredients in a bowl. Add rest of ingredients and mix well. Put in muffin tins (fill to the top) and bake for 20 min. (or 14 min. if using a mini muffin tin). [See Photos section.]

Blueberry-Lemon Quinoa Muffins (GF)

Thanks for the recipe, Tobi!

1 C quinoa flour
¾ C almond meal
⅓ C Xylitol (or raw honey, raw/organic agave, or Sucanat)
2½ tsp. baking powder (aluminum free)
¾ tsp. sea salt
1 egg (organic, range free), beaten
1 C plain yogurt
⅓ C coconut oil
½ - 1 tsp. lemon peel, freshly grated
¾ C blueberries (fresh or frozen)

Preheat oven to 400°. Grease muffin pan (or use paper liners if preferred). In a large bowl, combine quinoa flour, almond meal, Xylitol, baking powder, and sea salt. In a medium bowl, combine egg, plain yogurt, coconut oil, and lemon peel (make sure the egg, yogurt, and oil are at room temperature and warm enough when you do this, otherwise the coconut oil will solidify and not blend smoothly). Add the egg mixture to the flour mixture and stir until combined. Gently fold in the blueberries. Fill muffin pan cups to ⅔ full and bake until done (approximately 10 min., but varies depending on type of pan, pan size, and oven). Muffins are done when they are golden and a toothpick inserted into the center of one comes out clean. [See Photos section.]

Pancakes

Healthy Oatmeal Pancakes

Thanks for the recipe, Jane!

(Recipe was adapted by Robyn.)

It's easy to gradually convert to healthier and healthier eating. I started out doing half-and-half white flour to whole wheat flour, then gradually added more and more whole wheat until our family is at all whole wheat. Of course, each time I make these pancakes, I add different things, so they're a bit different every time. They are very filling and a great way to start out the day.

1½ - 2 C almond milk
¼ C coconut oil (liquid)
2 eggs (organic, free range)
1½ C whole-wheat flour
½ C rolled oats
1 Tbsp. baking powder (aluminum free)
½ tsp. cinnamon
¼ tsp. sea salt
optional: sliced bananas

Whisk wet ingredients together. Combine dry ingredients, then add to wet ingredients. Start out with 1½ C milk and add more if necessary.

Cook on a hot griddle. These take longer to cook through than traditional pancakes. We like to pour the batter, then put a layer of sliced bananas on top. Then when you flip the pancake, the bananas get cooked in. Serve with pure maple syrup. Top with optional yogurt sauce (plain yogurt, a dash of stevia, and some vanilla stirred together until smooth) and sliced strawberries or other berries.

Jan's Lumberjack Pancakes

Thanks for the recipe, Janelle!

(Recipe was adapted by Robyn.)

2 C rolled oats
1½ C whole-wheat flour
1 tsp. sea salt
½ C Sucanat or coconut palm sugar
2½ tsp. baking soda
2 C nut milk, at room temperature
3 eggs (organic, free range), beaten and at room temperature
2½ Tbsp. honey (raw)
3 Tbsp. coconut oil, warmed until liquid

Combine dry ingredients together. Add liquid ingredients and mix just until combined. Bake on hot griddle just a few minutes each side. These are sweet enough on their own that they can be eaten without any toppings! Or top with favorite pancake toppings and enjoy.

Green Pancakes

Thanks for the recipe, Kelly!

(Recipe was adapted by Robyn.)

1¼ C whole-wheat flour
2 tsp. baking powder (aluminum free)
¼ tsp. salt
3 Tbsp. raw honey or other natural sweetener
1 handful fresh spinach
½ banana
2 Tbsp. extra virgin coconut oil
1¼ C milk (rice, almond, or coconut), more or less, depending on how you like your pancakes
1 egg (organic, free range)
optional: 1 Tbsp. fresh lemon juice

Purée spinach and banana in a blender with ½ of the milk. Mix dry ingredients together, then add wet ingredients.

Gluten-Free Blender Pancakes (GF)

Thanks for the recipe, Lisa Fielding (KISforhealth.com)!

(Recipe was adapted by Robyn.)

1 C milk (almond, rice, or coconut)
1 C buttermilk
1 C brown rice kernels
½ C buckwheat kernels
½ C mixed quinoa, amaranth, chia, and flax
4 eggs (organic, free range)
1 tsp. baking powder (aluminum free)
2 tsp. sea salt
¼ C extra virgin olive oil
¼ C blackstrap molasses or raw honey

Blend rice and milk together for about 5 min. Add the brown rice, buckwheat, and ½ C quinoa mix and blend for a few more min. Add the rest if the ingredients and blend for 1 min. or until smooth. Cook on a skillet or hot fry pan.

> ***Tip:*** Can be saved in the fridge for a quick breakfast.

Protein- and Fiber-Packed Pancakes (GF)

Thanks for the recipe, Natasha!

½ C cottage cheese
½ C steel-cut oats [Use gluten-free oats for GF recipe.]
3 egg whites (organic, range free)
milk (almond, coconut, or rice), to get pancake consistency
1 Tbsp. ground flax seed
optional: 1 packet stevia

Mix all the ingredients together in a blender and continue to add milk until you get the mixture to a pancake batter consistency. Cook until browned on both sides. This batter make very filling and hearty pancakes. [See Photos section.]

> ***Tip:*** I like to add frozen blueberies or a mashed banana and nuts to create a few different varieties of pancakes.

Supper Pancakes (V)

Thanks for the recipe, Paula!

(Recipe was adapted by Robyn.)

1 C whole-grain pancake mix
1 C whole-wheat graham flour
optional: ½ C rolled oats
optional: ¼ C milled flaxseed
optional: a few pecans or walnuts, or even a bit of cinnamon

Make this just like regular pancakes. Mix with water only and fry on griddle.

Cereals & "Dairy"

Cereals

Baked Oatmeal (GF)

Thanks for the recipe, Andrea!

3 C rolled oats [Use gluten-free oats for GF recipe.]
1 C rapadura (we use ½ C) or Sucanat or coconut sugar
2 Tbsp. cinnamon
2 Tbsp. baking powder (aluminum free)
1 tsp. sea salt
1 C almond, coconut, or rice milk
2 eggs (organic and free range) *OR* 2 Tbsp. chia seeds soaked 20+ min. in 6 Tbsp. water
½ C melted coconut oil
2 Tbsp. vanilla extract
¾ dried cranberries

Preheat oven to 350°. Mix together all dry ingredients. Then beat in eggs, milk, oil, and vanilla. Fold in cranberries. Bake for 30-35 min.

Fruity Buckwheat Breakfast (R,V,GF)

Thanks for the recipe, Angel!

½ - ¾ C buckwheat
1 large apple
cinnamon (to taste)
1 banana

Soak the buckwheat overnight and rinse it thoroughly in the morning. Cut the apple into chunks and blend it with the buckwheat to the consistency you prefer. Add cinnamon and top it off with sliced banana. It's magically delicious!

Tip: The apple can be substituted for other fruit. When I use kiwi, I leave the cinnamon out. If I don't have any fresh fruit, I soak 3-4 dates overnight and mix them and the soaking water instead of the apple.

Raw Sweet Potato Cereal (R,V,GF)

Thanks for the recipe, Bethany Knighton!

I adapted this from a recipe by Wardeh at www.gnowfglins.com.

2 sweet potatoes (not yams), grated
1 C unsweetened medium-shredded coconut *OR* 2 C unsweetened large-flake coconut
1 C dried fruit of your choice (raisins, cranberries, dates, pears, etc.)
1 C chopped raw almonds or pecans or walnuts
2 tsp. cinnamon
garnishes: fresh or frozen fruit, raw honey or agave, raw nut milk

Toss all ingredients (except garnishes) together in a mixing bowl. Spoon into bowls. Garnish as desired. Cover leftovers and they will keep for several days in the fridge. [See Photos section.]

Ageless Beauty Oatmeal (V,GF)

Thanks for the recipe, Cathy Painter (author of TheAgelessBeautyReport.com)!

½ C cooked oatmeal (I love John McCann's Steel Cut Irish Oatmeal—avoid instant oats!) [Use gluten-free oats for GF recipe.]
2 Tbsp. raw coconut oil
¼ C dried raw goji berries
1 Tbsp. chopped raw chopped almonds

Mix all together and enjoy!

Apple-Cinnamon Oatmeal (V,GF)

Thanks for the recipe, Evi from Germany!

(Recipe was adapted by Robyn.)

1 C regular rolled oats [Use gluten-free oats for GF recipe.]
⅔ C apple juice concentrate
1⅓ C water
½ tsp. cinnamon
optional: ½ C raisins or currants

Combine oats, apple juice concentrate, water, and cinnamon in a saucepan. Bring to a simmer, then cover and cook 3 min. Remove from heat and stir in raisins or currants. Let stand 3 min. before serving. One of my favorite breakfasts!

Crock Pot Cornmeal Porridge (V,GF)

Thanks for the recipe, Evi from Germany!

1½ C medium- or coarse-ground cornmeal
5 C water
¾ tsp. sea salt
½ C slivered almonds, toasted
pure maple syrup
optional: ½ C chopped dates

Combine cornmeal, water, salt, and optional dates in a 3½-4 qt. slow cooker. Cover and cook on low for 6 hr. (overnight). When it is time to eat, stir in the almonds. (To toast the slivered almonds, put them in a dry skillet over medium heat, shake or stir until they are lightly browned, then remove from pan immediately.) Spoon porridge into bowls and drizzle with maple syrup. Talk about comfort food! *Makes 4 servings.*

Crock Pot Wheat Berries & Oats (V)

Thanks for the recipe, Evi from Germany!

½ C wheat berries
¼ C cracked wheat
½ C rolled oats or barley
1 tsp. cinnamon
dash sea salt
4 C water

Put all ingredients in a 3½-4 qt. slow cooker. Cover and cook on low for 6 hr. (if you do it overnight, it is ready to eat when you get up!). Stir in some dried cranberries or raisins and top with a little maple syrup and rice milk. A nice breakfast in the winter or an afternoon snack after a day in the snow. *Makes 4 servings.*

Breakfast Polenta Porridge (Two Ways) (V,GF)

Thanks for the recipe, Garon!

Note: Only Version 2 is vegan and gluten free!

Version 1:

1 C medium course-ground dried corn
3 C water
almond milk, to taste
raw honey, to taste

Bring water to boil and add ground corn, reduce heat to medium-low, and cook for 10 min., stirring occasionally. Serve with almond milk and honey.

Version 2:

1 C medium course-ground corn
2 C water
2 C almond milk or rice milk

Bring water and milk to boil and add ground corn, reduce heat to low, and cook for 30 min., stirring often.

Overnight Apple-Cinnamon Oatmeal (V,GF)

Thanks for the recipe, J!

Takes only 10 minutes of your time in the morning.

3 Tbsp. apple juice
½ tsp. cinnamon
1 apple, cored and finely diced
2 Tbsp. raisins
½ C water
½ C old-fashioned rolled oats [Use gluten-free oats for GF recipe.]
optional: 2 raw pecan halves, finely minced

In a small, sealable container, mix together apple juice and cinnamon. Add apple and raisins until combined, then seal and refrigerate to marinate overnight.

In a small bowl stir, together the water and oats. Cover with plastic wrap and let stand to soak overnight (at least 7 hr.) in order to neutralize phytic acid.

When marinating and soaking are complete, in a small pan bring water to a boil, add presoaked oats, and simmer on medium-low heat for 5 min., stirring frequently. Remove from heat. Add marinated fruit and optional nuts, then cover and let stand for 5 min. Mix well and serve immediately. *Makes 1 serving.*

Raw Breakfast Cereal (R,V,GF)

Thanks for the recipe, Jenna Strawn!

1 C steel cut oats [Use gluten-free oats for GF recipe.]
1½ C water
½ C raisins, or to taste
2 Gala (or other sweet) apple, chopped
2 bananas, chopped
optional: ¼ C raw sunflower seeds
optional: ¼ C raw pumpkin seeds
optional: ¼ C raw walnuts
optional: ¼ C raw almonds
optional: ¼ C raw pecans

Soak the oats, raisins, and any or all of the optional ingredients in the water overnight in a covered glass container (you might need to use more water if you use a lot of the optional ingredients). The optional ingredients are to add protein to the cereal. Use plastic wrap to cover it if container doesn't have a lid.

In the morning, take out the amount of cereal you want and add ½ chopped apple and ½ chopped banana to *each serving*. It is not necessary to sweeten or add milk to this cereal. It is moist and sweet because of the soaking water and added fruit. *Makes 3-6 servings*.

Note: You can add all of the chopped fruit for all of the servings to the cereal mixture after it has soaked overnight, so that you don't have to chop fruit each morning. If you do add all the chopped fruit on the first day, remember to add fruit fresh or some kind of ascorbic acid to the fruit when it is chopped so it will not turn yucky brown over the next couple of days that you are eating it. Always keep it in the refrigerator. This cereal is best when used in 3-4 days.

Mixed Whole-Grain Breakfast (V,GF)

Thanks for the recipe, Jody!

1 C water
2 Tbsp. buckwheat groats (raw, not toasted)
2 Tbsp. millet
3 Tbsp. quinoa
½ C chopped apple
¼ C chopped almonds (soak whole almonds overnight, then chop)
¼ C raisins
¼ tsp. cinnamon
⅛ tsp. cardamom
⅛ tsp. sea salt

Put buckwheat, millet, and quinoa in a strainer and rinse thoroughly. Put in a bowl and soak in some water for a few minutes, then drain. Bring water to a boil in a small pot. Stir in rinsed grains, apple, almonds, raisins, and spices. When simmering, cover and reduce heat to low. Cook 15 min. and then turn off heat and let the pot sit, covered, for another 5 min. Serve with almond milk. *Makes 2 servings*. [See Photos section.]

Raw Buckwheat "Granola" (R,V,GF)

Thanks for the recipe, Kathy Marsden!

2 qt. buckwheat (soaked overnight, rinsed, and drained)
1 C sprouted sesame seeds (soaked overnight, rinsed, and drained or sprouted)
1 C flax seeds (soaked overnight and drained)
1 pt. sunflower seeds (soaked overnight, rinsed, and drained) or more to taste
1 C pumpkin seeds (soaked overnight, rinsed, and drained)
1 pt. walnuts (soaked overnight, rinsed, and drained)
1 pt. almonds (soaked overnight, rinsed, and drained)
1 qt. raisins (soak in barely enough water to cover overnight and reserve soaking water)
1 qt. dates, chopped
4 apples *OR* 2-3 C raw applesauc
1 C raw honey or agave (or a combination) [Use only agave for V recipe.]
2 Tbsp. vanilla
optional: ⅓ lb. cacao nibs *OR* 4 squares unsweetened dark chocolate (organic Dagoba) *OR* ⅓ C carob, plus sweetener to taste
optional: sea salt, to taste

Blend dates and raisins with their soaking water (if adding the sweetened cacao/chocolate/carob, blend it in now so it gets ground up well). Add apples or applesauce to blender and blend. Add honey/agave and blend. Add vanilla and flax and blend again.

Mix all of the soaked grains, seeds, and nuts together and add the blended ingredients. I add sea salt to taste and adjust sweetening. Sometimes I use cinnamon or other spices. I frequently use this as a "use up the sprouts and stuff in the fridge" granola. If I am making it just for myself, I make it less sweet (fewer raisins and dates) and use stevia.

Dehydrate the mixture on fruit leather sheets (½" thick or less) until dry. After it is mostly dry to the touch, transfer it to mesh sheets to finish drying.

Breakfast Mix (R,V,GF)

Thanks for the recipe, Michael!

I prepare this in the evening to eat the next morning.

½ C ground flax seeds (grind just prior)
¼ C ground sesame seeds (grind just prior)
¼ C chia seeds
1 C chopped walnuts
½ C chopped cashews
½ C raisins
½ C sunflower seeds
water (distilled or filtered), enough for desired consistency
organic fruit in season, diced (pear, peach, strawberry, raspberry)

Mix together the dry ingredients with a spoon. Place in a small crock pot and pour in enough water so that the ingredients float. (Adjust the amount of water for your consistency preference.) Set temperature to 100º and soak overnight. (It is good without being heated as well.) Mix in fresh organic fruit in the morning, and it's ready to eat. *Serves 1 hungry man.*

Yummy Yam Breakfast (R,V,GF)

Thanks for the recipe, Paula!

Use whatever amounts you want of the following ingredients:

yams, shredded or pulse-chopped in food processor until fine
apples, shredded or pulse-chopped in food processor (or you could process them with a couple dates until it is applesauce; if you process it long enough, you can even leave in the apple seeds)
blueberries
raisins, soaked overnight
almonds, soaked overnight
sunflower seeds, soaked overnight
cinnamon

Rinse the almonds and sunflower seeds. You can leave the almonds whole, pulse, or chop them in the food processor. Mix all ingredients together, including the raisin soak water (it's sweet). You can add anything else you happen to have around or you can substitute any nut for the almonds. Be creative and enjoy!

Orange Chia Seed Breakfast Pudding (R,V,GF)

Thanks for the recipe, RHR!

¼ C raw almonds, soaked overnight, drained, and rinsed
1 C water
3 pitted dates, softened
juice of 2 oranges
1 orange (zest and fruit)
⅓ C chia seeds
optional: granola, for topping [Use gluten-free granola for GF recipe.]

Place almonds and water in high-powered blender. Process until well blended, then remove to nut milk bag and strain. Place almond milk back in blender with dates and blend until very smooth. Remove the zest from one orange and add to the almond milk/date mixture. Segment the insides of the orange and set aside. Juice the two remaining oranges and add juice (aprox. ½ - ¾ C) to the almond milk mixture. Stir. Add chia seeds and stir. Let set for 20 min. Stir in orange sections that you had set aside. Top with granola, if desired. *Makes 2 servings.*

Cinnamon Fruit Oatmeal (V,GF)

Thanks for the recipe, Tamara!

1 C water
1 tsp. vanilla extract
¼ tsp. cinnamon
½ C old-fashioned rolled oats [Use gluten-free oats for GF recipe.]
½ C blueberries
2 apples, chopped
2 Tbsp. chopped walnuts
1 Tbsp. ground flax seeds
optional: ¼ C raisins

In a saucepan, combine water with the vanilla and cinnamon and bring to a boil. Reduce heat to a simmer and stir in the oats. When the mixture starts to simmer, add the blueberries. Remove from the heat when the berries are heated through. Cover and let stand for 15 min. until thick and creamy. Mix in the apples, nuts, flax seeds, and optional raisins.

Milks & Creams

Whipped Coconut Cream (R,V,GF)

Thanks for the recipe, Aimee (www.aimeehenrikson.blogspot.com)!

1 can "full fat" organic coconut milk, chilled in the fridge for some time or overnight (best)
cinnamon, to taste
vanilla, to taste

Scoop out all the thickened coconut cream so that only water is left over. (Don't discard the water—use it to drink or in a shake!) After scooping it out, add a little cinnamon and vanilla and whip it in a mixing bowl until it thickens to desired consistency.

Raw Coconut Cream (R,V,GF)

Thanks for the recipe, Janet

1 C raw cashews or almonds
1 C water
1 C young coconut flesh (or shredded)
¼ C raw, organic agave
pinch sea salt

Blend all in high-speed blender until smooth. Delicious on top of oatmeal or granola.

Raw Cashew Cream (R,V,GF)

Thanks for the recipe, Juanique!

4 C raw, organic cashews

4-6 Tbsp. raw, organic agave (depending how sweet you want the cream)

1½ tsp. vanilla essence

1½ - 3 C water (depending how thick/thin you want the cream)

Toss all ingredients into a blender and blend until creamy. Eat with your favorite fruits such as strawberries, blueberries, mangos, and peaches. It's great for snacks and desserts, and any company that may come by is sure to love it!

Raw Cashew Cream Too (R,V,GF)

Thanks for the recipe, Linda (lindasgoldenyears.blogspot.com)!

Cashew cream is a vegan chef staple that stands in for dairy in a variety of ways. In the raw-food world where it originated, cashew cream is used in lots of desserts. When you cook with it, though, it can be so much more—from cheese filling in ravioli to heavy cream in soups.

The trick when making cashew cream is to use raw cashews. They have no flavor of their own; they're just a vessel for fat and creaminess. (It's the roasting that brings out the familiar sweetness in cashews.)

Because it has a nice fat content, cashew cream reduces in a pan even faster than heavy cream. (Soy milk, which some people use in vegan cooking, has no fat and so it doesn't reduce into a thick sauce—therefore, it's really not an alternative.)

2 C whole, raw cashews (not pieces, which are often dry), rinsed well under cold water

Put the cashews in a bowl and add enough cold water to cover them. Cover the bowl and refrigerate overnight. Drain the cashews and rinse under cold water. Place cashews in a blender with enough fresh cold water to cover them by 1". Blend on high for several minutes until very smooth. If you're not using a professional high-speed blender such as a VitaMix or Blendtec, which creates an ultra-smooth cream, strain the cashew cream through a fine-meshed sieve. *Makes about 2¼ C thick cream or 3½ C regular cream.* [See Photos section.]

Tip: It can be stored 2 to 3 days in the refrigerator and can be frozen for up to 6 months. But after it's defrosted it can be a bit lumpy, so it's good to give it a spin in the blender to smooth it out before using it.

Creamy Almond Milk (R,V,GF)

Thanks for the recipe, Pam (adapted from Hallelujah Acres)!

(Recipe was adapted by Robyn.)

⅔ C raw almonds, soaked overnight and drained
⅓ C unsweetened dried coconut
1 tsp. sea salt
1 C cooked brown rice
1 Tbsp. pure vanilla
2 Tbsp. raw honey or agave nectar [Use agave for V recipe.]

Blend the first three ingredients to "flour" in high-speed blender. Add the last three ingredients, then add water gradually until you have 2 qt. (64 oz.) of milk. Lasts about one week in the refrigerator.

"Cheeses"

Sliceable Cashew "Cheese" (R,V,GF)

Thanks for the recipe, Alina!

- 2 C water
- 3 Tbsp. agar flakes *OR* 3 tsp. agar powder
- 1 C raw cashews
- 2 Tbsp. pimentos *OR* ½ C diced red bell pepper
- 1 Tbsp. lemon juice
- 1 Tbsp. food yeast flakes
- 1½ tsp. salt
- ½ tsp. onion powder
- ¼ tsp. garlic powder

Boil together the agar and water for 1-2 min. Place in a blender with all the remaining ingredients and blend for 1-2 min. until very smooth. Pour into containers and chill. Slice when firm.

> ***Tip:*** This recipe makes a yellow cheese. Leave out the pimentos for white cheese. You can also add herbs like dill, parsley, chives, basil, etc. It can be frozen and it shreds best when partially frozen. It's great pizza or lasagna because it melts well.

Cashew "Cheese" (R,V,GF)

Thanks for the recipe, Sharon!

(Recipe was adapted by Robyn.)

- ½ C raw cashews, soaked for a few hours and drained
- ¼ C nutritional or Brewer's yeast
- 2 Tbsp. extra virgin olive oil
- 1 Tbsp. dulse flakes
- 1 clove garlic

Process the cashews to a fine meal in a food processor. Add yeast to cashews and process to combine. Drizzle in oil and blend for 1 min. Add the oil, dulse flakes, and garlic and blend until smooth.

Salsas, Sauces, & Relishes

Salsas

Best Fresh Salsa (R,V,GF)

Thanks for the recipe, Anna Cox!

½ bunch cilantro
½ small onion
1 Tbsp. lime juice
6 Roma tomatoes
1 Serrano pepper
1 tsp. white vinegar
1 tsp. sea salt

Pulse all except cilantro in food processor until desired chunkiness is achieved. Hand-chop cilantro for best consistency and mix in.

John's Salsa (R,V,GF)

Thanks for the recipe, John Andrews!

15 oz. organic tomato sauce
4 medium tomatoes
3 jalapeño peppers
5 Fresno peppers
1 Anaheim or Serrano pepper
1-1½ large sweet bell peppers (any color)
1 green onion
¼ C chopped sweet onion

Optional Herbs and Spices:
2-4 cloves crushed garlic
¼ tsp. cumin
1 tsp. chopped ginger root
1 tsp. horseradish (preferably freshly grated)
parsley (about 5 sprigs)
cilantro (at least 10 sprigs or a handful—hard to overdo the cilantro)
dash coriander amd/or paprika
1 Tbsp. chives
juice of ½ lime
½ tsp. oregano

Put the tomato sauce in the food processor first (otherwise the salsa will get a lot of air bubbles and appear foamy), then add all other ingredients and blend well. I make this weekly and love it.

Cabbage Salsa (R,V,GF)

Thanks for the recipe, Michelle!

1 small head green cabbage, chopped
2 large tomatoes, chopped
1-2 carrots, chopped
1 small red onion, chopped
¼ C cilantro, chopped
juice of 2 limes
2-3 Tbsp. pickled jalapeños, chopped, plus some of the pickling juice (depending how spicy you want it) [Use raw jalapeños for R recipe.]
1 tsp. extra virgin olive oil
1 Tbsp. rice wine vinegar
sea salt to taste
black pepper to taste

Combine all ingredients and let sit in refrigerator for at least 30 min. (if you can wait!). It's even better the next day.

I serve this as a dip with baked sprouted-wheat tortilla wedges or with refried beans on a wrap. Also great the next day for breakfast burritos, good on a salad, etc.

Kick N Mango Salsa (R,V,GF)

Thanks for the recipe, NutriMom Julia!

2 large mangos, peeled and chopped
¼ red onion, chopped
juice of 1 lime
2 Tbsp. fresh cilantro, chopped
⅛ tsp. Original Crystal Himalayan Salt
pinch cayenne
½ jalapeño pepper, seeded & chopped
1 clove garlic, minced

Mix all together and serve with blue corn-sesame tortilla chips or dehydrated corn chips, or use on tacos/burritos.

Mango Salsa (R,V,GF)

Thanks for the recipe, Paula!

2 mangos, peeled & diced
¼ C chopped red onion
¼ C diced red pepper
1 handful cilantro, chopped
juice of 1 lime
pinch sea salt

Mix all together and use like regular salsa, or serve tossed with brown rice and black or kidney beans. [See Photos section.]

Yummy Salsa (R,V,GF)

Thanks for the recipe, Paula!

6 ripe tomatoes, quartered
¼ C fresh cilantro
½ medium onion, halved
1 tsp. fresh lemon juice
1 Serrano chili pepper
1 tsp. raw apple cider vinegar
1 tsp. sea salt

Place first the tomatoes and then the other ingredients in a blender and secure the lid. Pulse several times.

Tip: Sometimes you need to alternate scraping the sides of the blender and pulsing.

Sauces

Simple "Cheese" Sauce (R,V,GF)

Thanks for the recipe, Alina!

1 C raw cashew nuts

2 C water

½ large (or 1 small) red bell pepper *OR* ¼ C canned pimentos or red peppers

1½ tsp. sea salt

2 tsp. onion powder

2 Tbsp. nutritional yeast flakes

½ tsp. garlic powder

Blend all until smooth, then heat to a boil, stirring until thick. Use for pizza, lasagna, burritos, etc. *Makes 3 cups.*

Sneaky Momma's Tomato Sauce (V,GF)

Thanks for the recipe, Brynna!

1 Tbsp. extra virgin olive oil
1 medium onion, chopped
1 sweet red pepper, chopped
2 garlic cloves, minced
1 (15 oz.) can diced tomatoes, drained
1 (15 oz.) can tomato sauce (low sodium if possible)
2 C kale leaves, shredded
1 large carrot, diced
1 Tbsp. dried parsley
1 Tbsp. Italian seasoning
pinch red pepper flakes
1 Tbsp. raw agave nectar
sea salt and pepper, to taste

Heat the olive oil in a wide saucepan over medium heat. Sauté the onion and red pepper until soft, about 5 minutes. Add the garlic and sauté, stirring constantly, for 1 more min.

Add everything else, except the agave, salt, and pepper, and stir until well blended. When the mixture begins to bubble, lower the heat and cook on low heat, stirring occasionally, for about 1 hour.

Let it cool slightly, then blend in high-speed blender until smooth (in two batches…the smoother the better). Put back on heat to rewarm and add agave, salt, and pepper. *Makes about 4 cups.*

Peanut Sauce (R,GF)

Thanks for the recipe, Donna (www.helplessvegetarian.com)!

1 tsp. fresh grated ginger
½ tsp. cayenne or chili powder (whatever works for your heat meter)
½ C peanut butter (preferably raw, organic) [Use raw p.b. for R recipe.]
½ C tamari (can add more if you like)
1½ Tbsp. raw honey
3 Tbsp. sesame oil
5-6 Tbsp. water

Whisk all ingredients until well blended. I like to serve it over collard rolls.

Cheez Sauce (V)

Thanks for the recipe, Evi from Germany!

(Recipe was adapted by Robyn.)

This sauce is good for macaroni-and-cheese casserole, with whole-grain pasta, or as a topping for lasagne or a pan of enchiladas.

½ C nutritional yeast flakes
½ C finely ground white-wheat, whole-wheat flour
1 tsp. sea salt
½ tsp. garlic powder
2 C water
¼ C extra virgin olive oil
1 tsp. prepared mustard

Mix yeast flakes, flour, salt, and garlic powder in a 2-qt. saucepan. Whisk in water. Cook over medium heat, whisking until mixture thickens and bubbles. Cook 30 sec. more, then remove from heat and whisk in oil and mustard. Sauce will thicken as it cools, but will thin when heated. [See Photos section.]

Green Enchilada Sauce (V,GF)

Thanks for the recipe, Jennifer D.!

7-8 tomatillos (because they are small)
1 yellow or orange tomato
1 avocado
1 clove garlic
½ small onion
1 jalapeño (if you get a small one, it won't be hot)
some cilantro
juice of ½ lime
optional: pinch sea salt

Remove the thin peel from the tomatillos, then boil them for 10 min. Then put all ingredients into a blender and blend.

This is an enchilada sauce, but I love to drink it warm—just a cup. It is so flavorful! [See Photos section.]

Sun-Dried Tomato Pesto (R,V,GF)

Thanks for the recipe, Lisa!

2 C fresh basil

4-5 halves sun-dried tomatoes (soaked in water for at least 10 min. to soften)

4 cloves garlic, peeled

½ C extra virgin olive oil

In a blender, add the fresh basil, sun-dried tomatoes, and garlic. Blend on medium. While blending, slowly add the olive oil through the hole of the blender lid until fully incorporated. *Makes 4-6 servings (about 2-3 cups).* [See Photos section.]

Relishes

Cranberry Relish (R,V,GF)

Thanks for the recipe, Jenna Strawn!

1 lb. raw, whole cranberries
2 C sweetener of choice
1 C pecans
3 oranges, with some rind
1-2 apples, cored and seeded but with peels

Grind all ingredients together and let sit for several hours in the refrigerator before using. We eat this every year at Thanksgiving and Christmas. Yum!

Tip: Do not use a food processor "S" blade (Bosch food processor is OK), but a salad shooter is good. Grind the oranges first, then grind the orange peel with the apples.

Mixed Whole-Grain Breakfast (V,GF) (page 30)

Raw Sweet Potato Cereal (R,V,GF) (pagc 25)

Raw Cashew Cream (R,V,GF) (page 35)

Protein- and Fiber-Packed Pancakes (GF) (page 20)

Blueberry-Lemon Quinoa Muffins (GF) (page 17)

Pumpkin Muffins (V) (page 17)

Soda Bread (page 4)

Yummy Cornbread (page 4)

Cheez Sauce (V) (page 46)

Sun-Dried Tomato Pesto (R,V,GF) (page 47)

Green Enchilada Sauce (V,GF) (page 46)

Mango Salsa (R,V,GF) (page 43)

Oatmeal Cookies (GF) (page 79)

Raw Macaroon Cookies (R,V,GF) (page 78)

Peanut Butter Cups (R,V,GF) (page 77)

Jonni Sue's Almond-Peanut Butter Bars (R,V,GF) (page 76)

Almond Power Bars (V,GF) (page 74)

Coconut Granola Bars (page 66)

Passionate Parsnip Chips (R,V,GF) (page 94)

Best "Cheesy" Kale Chips (R,V,GF) (page 93)

Vanilla Butter Apple Dip (V,GF) (page 101)

Cinnamon-Vanilla Pecan Butter (R,V,GF) (page 101)

“Cheesy” Chickpeas (V,GF) (page 106)

Hansel and Gretel Mix (R,V,GF) (page 106)

Sweet Candied Nuts (GF) (page 105)

Hot Chocolate (R,V,GF) (page 162)

Blushing Bunny (R,V,GF) (page 155)

Grape-Coconut Smoothie (V,GF) (page 132)

Pumpkin Berry Bliss (V,GF) (page 131)

Grapefruit Sunrise (R,V,GF) (page 115)

Greena Colada (R,V,GF) (page 155)

Lemon-Ginger Tonic Blast (R,V,GF) (page 148)

Snacks

Cookies, Candy, Bars, & Balls

Coconut Granola Bars

Thanks for the recipe, Amber Bodily!

4 C rolled oats (uncooked)
1 C Sucanat or coconut palm sugar
1 tsp. vanilla extract
½ tsp. ground cinnamon
½ C shredded coconut
1 C chopped nuts (any kind)
¾ C melted coconut oil
½ C raw honey
⅔ C natural peanut butter
¼ C wheat germ

Preheat oven to 450°. Combine all ingredients in a large bowl and mix well. Press into a well greased 15½"x10½" jelly roll pan. Bake for 8-10 min. When cooled, store in an airtight container to keep them chewy. *Makes 20 bars*. [See Photos section.]

Granola Bars (GF)

Thanks for the recipe, Bobbi!

2 C rolled oats [Use gluten-free oats for GF recipe.]
¾ C wheat germ or oat bran [Use gluten-free bran for GF recipe.]
¾ C sunflower seeds or walnuts
1 C crushed peanuts or pumpkin seeds
2 C puffed rice (for a soft bar)

Spread the above ingredients onto a large, dry cookie sheet/roasting pan and toast them in the oven. While dry ingredients are toasting, line 8"x13" pan with foil and spray with olive oil nonstick spray. (If you double the recipe, use a large cookie sheet and line with foil and spray.)

Measure out 8 oz. of dried fruits (such as any of the following) and put in a container ready to mix quickly when dry ingredients come out of oven:

Craisins
Golden raisins
Dry blueberries
Dates (chopped)

In your very largest pan (to mix all in at the end), heat and mix until just melted:

⅓ C natural peanut butter
⅓ C raw agave syrup
½ C raw local honey
4 Tbsp. cold-pressed coconut oil
⅓ tsp. sea salt
1-2 Tbsp. vanilla (not added until mixture removed from heat!)

Remove from heat and mix in vanilla. Pour out on foil-lined pan. Use a second piece of foil to press down hard. Chill 2 - 3 hours. Cut into bars, put into snack bags, and freeze—or press into ice cube trays, freeze, and pop out when frozen!

Chocolate Fudge (R,V,GF)

Thanks for the recipe, Brenda!

6 Tbsp. raw agave
6 oz. raw nut butter (any nut)
2 oz. sesame seeds
2 oz. sunflower seeds (soaked, if preferred)
1 oz. cacao powder
1 oz. shredded coconut (no sugar added)
1 oz. raisins or sultanas (soaked briefly, if preferred)

Use a food processor to mix the agave and nut butter first. Then add the other ingredients except for the raisins/sultanas either by hand or briefly in the food processor (the seeds need to remain as intact as possible). Press mixture into a dish which has been greased very slightly with coconut oil. Finally, press the raisins/sultanas on top of the mixture. Refrigerate until ready to be enjoyed!

Tip: Alternatively, you could roll the mixture into large balls and coat with sesame seeds, cacao powder, or coconut flakes. Eat as an energy ball!!

Peanut Butter Almond Balls

Thanks for the recipe, Catherine (from her book, Catherine's Recipes*)!*

I make this recipe as a "by-product" of making almond milk with my raw almonds. First I describe how I make almond milk below. My family likes it strained, and I use the almond meal that I strain out to make these cookies.

Almond Milk:

- 1 C raw almonds
- 2 C water
- enough water to make ½ gallon
- 15 drops stevia
- 1 tsp. vanilla extract

Place almonds in a blender with 2 C water and blend well. Strain this and save the almond meal for the cookie recipe below. To finish making the almond milk, add enough water to the "milk" to make ½ gallon, then add stevia and vanilla.

Cookies:

- 1 C almond meal (from making almond milk; see above)
- 1 C creamy, natural peanut butter
- 1 C raw honey or agave [Use agave for V recipe.]
- 2 C oats or use shredded raw coconut in place of some or all of the oats [Use gluten-free oats for GF recipe.]
- 1 C rice protein powder or hemp protein power (I usually use chocolate)
- 1-2 Tbsp. raw cocoa

Combine the almond meal, peanut butter, and honey/agave in a food processor and blend. Add the remaining ingredients and blend as well as you can. I usually finish mixing this in bowl, and mix with a spoon or with my hands. Chill for about 30 min. in the fridge. Then form into balls with a small cookie scoop. Place cocoa in a small, fine strainer and lightly dust over the cookie balls.

Raw Brownie Balls (R,V,GF)

Thanks for the recipe, Darlene!

2 C raw walnuts, soaked and dehydrated
¾ C dates, pitted
2 Tbsp. raw cacao powder
dash sea salt

Mix all ingredients in food processor until mixture holds together when pressed between your fingers. Roll into balls, chill, and enjoy!

Almond Joyfuls (R,V,GF)

Thanks for the recipe, Desirée Hancock (www.unconventionalkitchen.com)!

These are so cute if you make them in the flexible molds from Ikea—they pop out easily and you can make them in fun shapes like hearts for Valentine's. Just put a little sauce in the bottom of the mold, freeze until hard, put the almond mixture on top, then freeze again until hard. I also make them with a cookie scoop for cute little mounds.

3 C shredded coconut
1½ C almond meal
1 C maple syrup
⅓ C coconut oil
1 Tbsp. vanilla
½ tsp. sea salt

Mix together all of the ingredients, then scoop out onto a cookie tray and freeze. While the cookies are freezing, make the chocolate sauce (below). Drizzle the chocolate sauce over the Almond Joyfuls.

Chocolate Sauce:

¾ C coconut oil
½ C cocoa powder
1 Tbsp. vanilla
¼ C agave

Soften the coconut oil, then add the cocoa powder, vanilla, and agave and whisk together until the ingredients are completely incorporated.

Gluten-Free Peanut Butter Cookies (GF)

Thanks for the recipe, Desirée Hancock (www.unconventionalkitchen.com)!

1 C creamy peanut butter (I like Adams)
1 C Sucanat or coconut palm sugar plus, more for rolling the cookies in
1 large egg (organic, free range), lightly beaten with a fork
1 tsp. baking powder
1 tsp. vanilla extract
optional: ¼ C chopped roasted peanuts

Preheat oven to 350°. Line two baking sheets with parchment paper or silicon baking liners.

In a large bowl, mix the peanut butter with 1 C sugar. Stir until well blended. Add the egg, baking powder, and vanilla and stir well. Pour some additional sugar in a small bowl. Take 1 Tbsp. of dough and roll into a ball. Roll the dough ball in the sugar and place on prepared baking sheet. Repeat with the rest of the dough.

Take a dinner fork, stick it in the sugar, and gently press it down on each dough ball to flatten, then turn the fork 90° and gently press again, making the traditional hatch markings of a peanut butter cookie.

Bake for 10 min. Take out of oven and let them cool on the baking sheet for 5 min. Gently transfer the cookies to a rack to finish cooling. *Makes 2 dozen cookies.*

Vegan Pumpkin Cookies & Variation (V)

Thanks for the recipe, Desirée Hancock (www.unconventionalkitchen.com)!

1 C agave (raw, organic)
½ C coconut oil
1 tsp. vanilla
¼ tsp. sea salt
1 C pumpkin, canned or fresh
2¼ C soft white wheat flour
1 tsp. baking soda
1 tsp. baking powder
2 tsp. cinnamon
½ tsp. freshly ground nutmeg
optional: 1 C chocolate chips (look for naturally sweetened ones)

Preheat oven to 350°. Mix the agave, coconut oil, and vanilla together until creamy. Mix all the dry ingredients together in a separate bowl, then add the dry mixture to the wet mixture and mix well. Fold in the chocolate chips. For uniform cookies, use a cookie scoop to drop the dough onto a cookie sheet and bake for 11-14 min. *Makes 2-3 dozen cookies.*

***Variation*: Cranberry-Walnut Pumpkin Cookies**

To the dry mixture above, add:

½ C chopped walnuts
¼ tsp. freshly ground nutmeg
optional: replace chocolate chips with ¾ C dried cranberries or white chocolate chips

Raw Brownies (R,V,GF)

Thanks for the recipe, Emily!

1 C dates
1 C raisins
½ C raw cocoa or carob powder
2 C raw walnuts
¼ C raw agave nectar or honey [Use agave for V recipe.]

Chop walnuts finely in a food processor. Add dates, raisins, and cocoa/carob powder and mix ingredients well. Add agave/honey and mix again. Press into a small, square baking pan and freeze for about 1 hr. Slice brownies into whatever sized pieces desired. Store in fridge or freezer.

No-Bake Chocolate Oatmeal Cookies (V,GF)

Thanks for the recipe, Evi from Germany!

(Recipe was adapted by Robyn.)

I usually double the recipe as these are normally gone quick.

⅔ C real maple syrup
¼ C coconut oil
5 Tbsp. unsweetened cocoa powder
1 tsp. ground cinnamon
½ C natural peanut or almond butter
2 C regular rolled oats [Use gluten-free oats for GF recipe.]
1 tsp. vanilla extract

In a saucepan over medium heat, combine the maple syrup, oil, cocoa, and cinnamon. Boil for 3 min., stirring constantly. Remove from heat and stir in the peanut butter, rolled oats, and vanilla until well blended. Drop by heaping spoonfuls onto waxed paper and chill to set, about 30 min. *Makes 2 dozen cookies.*

Nutty Brownie Balls (R,V,GF)

Thanks for the recipe, Evi from Germany!

1 C raw walnuts
1 C dates, pitted
¼ - ⅓ C cocoa or raw cacao powder
optional: vanilla and sea salt, to taste
optional: shredded coconut

Grind walnuts in food processor, then add rest of ingredients until well mixed. Roll into small balls, then optionally roll balls in coconut. Store in fridge or freezer.

Tip: You can also place mixture in a pan, sprinkle with optional coconut, press flat, and cut into brownie bars.

Almond Power Bars (V,GF)

Thanks for the recipe, Heidi!

2 C almonds, soaked and dehydrated
¼ C flax, chia, or pumpkin seeds
¼ C sesame seeds
½ C prunes, dates, or raisins
½ C shredded coconut
½ tsp. sea salt
2 Tbsp. coconut oil
3 Tbsp. coconut butter
½ C nut butter
1 Tbsp. real maple syrup or raw honey [Use maple syrup for V recipe.]
2-3 tsp. vanilla
½ C chocolate chips (naturally sweetened, from health food store) [Use dairy-free chips for V recipe.]

Combine the first six ingredients and pulse until rough chopped. Separately combine the coconut oil, coconut butter, and nut butter and heat over low heat until melted. Add the maple syrup/honey and vanilla to the melted oils first, *then* mix with the roughly pulsed mixture. Press into 8"x8" pan.

Place the chocolate chips in the still-hot pan used for melting oils and let sit until melted. Spread the melted chocolate over the mixture in pan. Refrigerate for 30 min. or until chocolate hardens. Remove from refrigerator, cut into bars, and serve. Store in refrigerator or freeze for later enjoyment! *Makes about 12-15 bars*. [See Photos section.]

Frozen Coconut Cookies (R,V,GF)

Thanks for the recipe, Jill Farris!

1 C virgin coconut oil

1 C dried unsweetened coconut (or more, if you want them really thick with coconut!)

few dashes kelp

2 tsp. (or more) real maple syrup

Stir coconut oil and coconut together until well mixed. Add rest of ingredients and mix well. Place spoonfuls of the mixture onto a wax-paper-covered cookie sheet and freeze. Eat frozen or partially thawed. (If you thaw them all the way they are too oily.) Enjoy!

Tip: There are lots of varieties to this recipe…you could add a dash of carob/cocoa powder or other flavorings!

Frozen Coconut Love Pats (V,GF)

Thanks for the recipe, Jill Farris!

1 C virgin coconut oil

1 C dried pure coconut

raw honey or coconut palm sugar, to taste [Use coconut palm sugar for V recipe.]

optional, for variations: cocoa or carob, chocolate chips or carob chips, more coconut [Use dairy-free chips for V recipe.]

Blend all together thoroughly. This mixture can be frozen in spoonful sizes on a piece of waxed paper and then stored in a Ziploc bag in the freezer. When frozen, these are very easy to eat and children love them too.

Jonni Sue's Almond-Peanut Butter Bars (R,V,GF)

Thanks for the recipe, Jonni Sue!

2 C raw almonds
½ C flax meal (ground flax seeds)
½ C unsweetened shredded coconut
½ C organic or natural peanut butter [Use raw p.b. for R recipe.]
½ tsp. sea salt
½ C coconut oil
4 drops liquid stevia
1 Tbsp. raw agave nectar
1 Tbsp. vanilla extract
½ C chopped dried fruit (raisins, dates, apricots, etc.)

Place almonds, flax meal, shredded coconut, peanut butter, and salt in a food processor and pulse about 10 sec. In a small sauce pan, melt coconut oil over very low heat. Remove coconut oil from stove and stir in stevia, agave, and vanilla. Add coconut oil mixture to ingredients in food processor and pulse only until a coarse paste forms. Remove mixture from processor an fold in dried fruit. Press mixture into a square glass baking dish and chill in refrigerator for 1 hour, until mixture hardens. Cut into bars and serve. [See Photos section.]

Chocolate Mints (R,V,GF)

Thanks for the recipe, Judy!

½ C organic, cold-pressed coconut oil
¼ C raw cocoa powder
¼ C raw agave nectar
3 drops mint flavor
optional: ⅛ C finely chopped almonds (soaked and dried first, if you like)

Mix all ingredients with whisk on low heat until oil is melted. Spoon or pour into bon-bon cups on a cookie sheet and freeze for 15 min. Store in a Ziploc bag or other container in the refrigerator.

Tip: On a cold winter night, make a cup of hot chocolate and melt a couple of these mints in it!

Peanut Butter Cups (R,V,GF)

Thanks for the recipe, Judy Gilmore!

½ C coconut oil (cold-pressed gives stronger coconut taste)
¼ C raw cocoa powder
¼ C raw agave nectar
peanut butter or almond butter, to taste [Use raw nut butter for R recipe.]

Mix first three ingredients with whisk on low heat until oil is melted. Pour small amount in bon-bon cups on cookie sheet and put in freezer for 4-5 min. Put a dab of peanut butter or almond butter on each and cover with more chocolate mixture to top of cup. Put in freezer for 10 more min. Store in Ziploc bags or container in the refrigerator. [See Photos section.]

Apricot Balls (R,V,GF)

Thanks for the recipe, Kim!

½ C chopped dried apricots
¼ C desiccated (dried) coconut
¼ C almond powder

Blend coconut and almond powser so that coconut becomes powdered. Add apricots and blend. Roll into balls.

Raw Almond Cookies (R)

Thanks for the recipe, Kristina!

1 C almond meal (use the pulp that remains from making almond milk)
1 tsp, ground cinnamon
pinch sea salt
⅓ C walnuts, crushed
2 Tbsp. honey
2 Tbsp. raw peanut butter or raw tahini, softened
1 handful raisins
1 handful sunflower seeds
1 Tbsp. coconut oil, melted

Mix all ingredients in a bowl until well combined. Roll into balls. Keep in freezer unless consuming within several days. If rolled small enough, they are fun to pop in your mouth frozen!

Nature's Knockout Raw Macaroon Cookies (R,V,GF)

Thanks for the recipe, Laurie & Tiffany!

2 C raw, organic almonds
2 C organic unsweetened shredded coconut
⅓ C extra virgin coconut oil
⅓ C raw agave nectar
¼ tsp. sea salt
½ tsp. pure vanilla extract

Mix all ingredients in a food processor. Drop by spoofuls onto cookie sheet, cover, and refrigerate for 1 hour.

Raw Macaroon Cookies (R,V,GF)

Thanks for the recipe, Laurie & Tiffany!

2 C raw organic almonds
2 C organic unsweetened coconut
⅓ C extra virgin coconut oil
⅓ C raw agave nectar
¼ tsp. sea salt
½ tsp. pure vanilla extract

Mix all ingredients in food processor. Spoon onto cookie sheet, cover, and refrigerate for an hour. [See Photos section.]

Oatmeal Cookies (GF)

Thanks for the recipe, Linda Ottley (www.lindasgoldenyears.blogspot.com)!

¾ C raw agave
½ C butter
½ C coconut oil (not melted)
2 organic, free-range eggs (or 2 yolks + 2 Tbsp. flaxseed soaked for 20 min. in 6 Tbsp. water)
1 tsp. baking soda
1 tsp. cinnamon *OR* 1-2 drops cinnamon (doTERRA essential oil)
1 tsp. vanilla *OR* 3-4 drops wild orange (doTERRA essential oil)
½ tsp. salt
1½ tsp. xanthan gum
½ C oat flour [Use gluten-free flour for GF recipe.]
½ C chickpea flour
3 C rolled oats [Use gluten-free oats for GF recipe.]
1 C raisins *OR* 1 C chocolate chips *OR* 3 bars "Nature's Sweet Life" Xylitol-sweetened dark chocolate, chopped
1 C chopped pecans

Preheat oven to 350°. Cream together agave, butter, coconut oil, and eggs. Add baking soda, spices, salt, and xanthium gum and mix. Then add oat flour, chickpea flour, and rolled oats and mix. Finally, stir in raisins and chopped pecans. Refrigerate dough for 1 hour (*very important*). Drop in rounded spoonfuls on cookie sheet and bake for 8 min. [See Photos section.]

Coco-Nutty No-Bake Cookies (GF)

Thanks for the recipe, Lisa (www.trainwithlisa.com)!

½ C organic, natural peanut or almond butter
¾ C oat flour [Use gluten-free flour for GF recipe.]
¾ C old-fashioned oats [Use gluten-free oats for GF recipe.]
¼ C unsweetened shredded coconut
¼ C raw agave
1-2 Tbsp. cocoa (depending how chocolaty you want them)
optional: additional ¼ C unsweetened shredded coconut (to roll cookies in)

Put all ingredients in a big bowl (or KitchenAid). Mix until all ingredients are well blended. Shape into small balls and roll in additional coconut, if you like. Store in an airtight container in the fridge.

Chocolaty Coconut-Oatmeal Cookies (GF)

Thanks for the recipe, Melissa!

Bring to just melted in a pot on the stove:

½ C organic butter or coconut oil
½ C coconut milk
¾ - 1 C raw honey
⅓ C cocoa powder (preferably raw)

Then add:

¾ C organic peanut butter
1 tsp. vanilla
1 C plain shredded coconut
2½ C rolled oats [Use gluten-free oats for GF recipe.]

Lay a sheet of wax paper on a cookie sheet. Drop the mixture by teaspoonful on the sheet and put in fridge to harden. Or just eat it hot by the spoonful! It's just too good!

Raw Lemon Cookies (R,GF)

Thanks for the recipe, Michael & RaeVern!

4 C raw cashews (soaked 4 hours or more)
½ C raw honey
zest of 1 large organic lemon
juice of 1 large organic lemon (about ¼ C)
1 C shredded dried coconut

Drain cashews and put into a food processor. Add honey to cashews. Zest lemon and add half the zest to the processor. Cut lemon in half, remove seeds, and squeeze juice from both halves into the food processor. Pulse a few times, scrape sides of the processor, and continue to pulse/scrape until a dough forms. Then add other half of lemon zest and the coconut (distribute it well; don't leave in a clump). Repeat pulse/scrape process until dough becomes a little chunky.

Add dough to a cookie press with any design, press cookies onto a Para-Flex, and dehydrate at 105° for 12 hours. Then remove Para-Flex and continue to dehydrate on mesh for another hour to make sure bottoms are not sticky.

Macaroons (V,GF)

Thanks for the recipe, Michelle!

(Recipe was adapted by Robyn.)

3 C dried, unsweetened coconut flakes

1½ C raw almonds, sprouted then ground into a fine powder in a high-speed blender

1 C real maple syrup

⅓ C coconut cream concentrate

1 Tbsp. vanilla extract

½ tsp. Original Crystal Himalayan Salt

optional: ¼ C cocoa powder for chocolate macaroons

Mix all ingredients well in a bowl. Drop by large spoonfuls onto racks in a dehydrator and heat at 105° for about 24 hours, until crunchy on the outside. Eat as cookie dough, refrigerate, or freeze for later.

Almond-Walnut-Date Bars (R,V,GF)

Thanks for the recipe, Mike!

1 C raw, organic almonds, ground

13 Medjool dates (pits removed), chopped

⅓ C organic walnuts, ground

1 Tbsp. flax seeds, ground

2 Tbsp. raw, organic agave nectar

1 Tbsp. organic blackstrap molasses

crushed hemp seeds (blended in high-speed blender)

wax paper

bowl of clean, cool water (for wax paper)

Place almonds, walnuts, and flax seeds into blender and blend until a flour. Mix dates with the nut/seed flour in a mixing bowl. Add agave and molasses and mix thoroughly. Refrigerate mixture for 5 min. With a wet spoon, scoop out desired amount and place on wet wax paper. Fold wax paper over and roll mixture into balls.

Sprinkle crushed hemp seeds onto a plate and roll balls in hemp until covered. Refrigerate in an air-tight container for at least 10 min. before eating.

Mahler Vanilla Pecan Protein Cookies (R,V,GF)

Thanks for the recipe, Mike Mahler (www.mikemahler.com)!

- 2 scoops Vanilla Sunwarrior Protein Powder
- 2 scoops Chocolate Sunwarrior Protein Powder (60 grams of high-quality protein and iron)
- 3 Tbsp. almond butter (good protein, fat, and magnesium)
- 3 Tbsp. flax powder (Omega-3, fiber; increases ratio of good estrogens to bad)
- ¼ C pecans
- ¼ C goji berries (high in vitamin A, vitamin C, and iron)
- 1 Tbsp. ginger powder (immune system, stomach health, and digestion)
- 1Tbsp. pumpkin pie spice (loaded with healthy spices)
- 1 Tbsp. cinnamon (increases insulin sensitivity and glucose regulation)
- 1 tsp. stevia
- 1½ C water

Preheat oven to 425°. Mix everything well in a bowl with a spoon until a thick paste forms. Taste to check seasoning. Divide into 8 cookies and place on cookie sheet. Bake for 15 min.

Nutritional Profile (each cookie):

- Protein: 10.4 grams
- Carbs: 8.6 grams
- Fat: 4.1 grams

Healthy No-Bake Cookies (V,GF)

Thanks for the recipe, Nina!

These are a quick, easy classic. When I changed my old recipe for more healthy ingredients, I was shocked that my family never even noticed the difference and actually complimented me and asked why they were so good!

½ C coconut oil

¼ - ½ C cocoa powder, non-alkalized and unsweetened (depending on how "chocolaty" you want them)

1 C organic, raw agave

1-2 tsp. real vanilla extract

1 C sliced almonds, walnuts, or raw pumpkin seeds (if your family doesn't like nuts, you can grind them to "hide" them, offering the health benefit without anyone knowing they're there!)

½ - 1 C natural peanut butter (depends on how much of the flavor you want)

3-4 C rolled oats (not "quick oats") [Use gluten-free oats for GF recipe.]

optional: ½ - 1 C of those great GreenSmoothieGirl group-buy dates (chopped), if your family likes the cookies a little sweeter

Slowly and carefully heat the coconut oil and agave until it just starts to bubble, then remove from heat—these are not cooked, just heated to incorporate ingredients. Stir in dates if you are using them. Then stir in cocoa powder, vanilla, and peanut butter until all ingredients are well incorporated, melted, and smooth. Stir in nuts and oats. Use a cookie scoop or spoon and drop cookie-sized portions on a cookie sheet lined with wax paper or parchment. Allow to cool, then enjoy.

Tip: For a more butterscotch flavor and for those who don't want chocolate, omit the cocoa powder and instead use full 1 C peanut butter; also, replace the agave with real maple syrup. The butterscotch version is best with walnuts or pecans. You might have to stir in a few extra oats as a result of omitting the cocoa powder. The glycemic index is higher because of the maple syrup, but it makes a nice alternative version.

Chocolate Cheat Eats (V,GF)

Thanks for the recipe, Nona!

1 C natural peanut butter (e.g., Adam's peanut butter)
1 tsp. cocoa (unsweetened, non-alkalized)
1 Tbsp. raw agave
¼ C chia seeds
2 Tbsp. coconut oil
1 C raisins
1 C sprouted raw almonds

Stir together all but raisins and almonds, then add them once other ingredients are well mixed. Roll mixture into balls or flatten and cut into bars.

Tip: The coconut oil can be left in little white chunks and your tastebuds will delight at finding them as you indulge.

Raw Vegan Protein Bars (V,GF)

Thanks for the recipe, Olga Cohen!

2 C whole raw almonds
¼ C ground golden flax seed
1 scoop Sun Warrior Protein Powder (chocolate)
½ C organic unsweetened coconut flakes
½ C organic almond butter
½ tsp. sea salt
½ C organic coconut oil, melted
1 Tbsp. organic maple syrup
2 tsp. vanilla
1 handful 100% baking chips *OR* 3-4 unsweetened chocolate baking squares, melted [Use dairy-free for V recipe.]
optional: 5 drops liquid stevia
optional: ½ C organic dates

Place almonds, flax seed, optional dates, coconut, almond butter, and salt in a food processor. Pulse to combine. In a small sauce pan, melt coconut oil using *low* heat. Remove from heat and add vanilla and maple syrup. Add melted oil mixture to food processor and pulse/grind ingredients until a coarse paste forms. Scoop out mixture and press down hard into a square bar brownie pan (with dividers).

Melt chocolate completely in a double boiler, then add optional stevia. Pour melted chocolate on top of pressed-down bars. Smooth out and place into fridge or freezer until chocolate has hardened. To serve, take bars out of fridge/freezer for at least 30 min. Work a knife around the edges gently and pop out bars onto pieces of plastic wrap. Wrap and freeze for later or munch right away!

Healthy Grain-Free Brownies (GF)

Thanks for the recipe, Ranae!

2 C black beans
3 lightly beaten eggs (organic, range free) OR 3 Tbsp. chia seeds soaked 20+ min. in 9 Tbsp. water)
⅓ C melted coconut oil
¼ C cocoa powder (non-dutched / non-alkalized)
⅛ tsp. sea salt
2 tsp. vanilla
½ C raw honey
½ C chopped bittersweet chocolate
⅓ C raw walnuts

Preheat oven to 350°. Blend all but chocolate and nuts until smooth. Fold in chocolate and nuts by hand. Bake brownie pan for 30 min.

Coco Bars (R,V,GF)

Thanks for the recipe, RB in CA!

2 C raw almonds (not soaked)
¼ C cacao beans
½ C raw agave syrup
¼ C dried coconut flakes

Put almonds and cacao beans in a food processor and process into a fine meal. Transfer to a bowl, add agave, and mix together into a dough. Add coconut flakes and mix again. Press in to a 9"x9" pan and cut into 16 equal-sized bars. Freezing in an airtight container helps keep the mixture together and makes it last for a few weeks.

Bonkers Rawdechox Bars (R,V,GF)

Thanks for the recipe, Robyn (not GreenSmoothieGirl—a different Robyn)!

1 C cacao nibs
1 C raw carob powder
½ C Pure Synergy
¼ C raw agave nectar
1 C grated raw cacao butter
1 tsp. purple corn extract
½ tsp. natural vitamin C powder

Add everything to a blender and blend until smooth. Pour into any mold and put in the fridge to set. You need only a small amount of this chocolate daily to get mega antioxidants into you for the detox magic to work!

Super-Chocolate Goji Lemon Bars (R,V,GF)

Thanks for the recipe, Robyn (not GreenSmoothieGirl—a different Robyn)!

2 C goji berries
2 C cacao nibs
1 tsp. lemon peel
2 C grated raw cacao butter

Add everything to a blender and blend until smooth. Pour into any mold and put in the fridge to set. Cut into bars to serve.

Toby Roamed Chocolate Bars (R,V,GF)

Thanks for the recipe, Robyn (not GreenSmoothieGirl—a different Robyn)!

½ C raw cacao nibs
2 C raw cacao butter
¼ C raw carob powder
1 dessert spoonful Pure Synergy
¼ C raw agave nectar
1 tsp. Blue Manna powder
1 tsp. maca
2 dessert spoonfuls coconut oil
½ C cashews

Grind the cacao nibs into a fine powder. Grind the cashews into a fine powder. Grate the white cacao butter and add to a bowl. Pour some warm water into another bowl and sit the bowl with the butter into this bowl. Don't get water into your cacao butter! Wait until the butter has melted, then add the other ingredients. Stir very well, then pour mixture into any pretty molds.

This is so much like that triangular chocolate that we all love. Er…except this one's got masses of brain food in it!

Lemon-Raspberry Thumbprint Cookies

Thanks for the recipe, Saskia!

1 C whole-wheat pastry flour
1 C almonds, ground into a fine meal
2 tsp. baking powder
1 Tbsp. lemon zest
½ tsp. sea salt
10 Tbsp. unsalted butter, melted
½ C real maple syrup
2 tsp. almond extract
½ tsp. lemon extract
raspberry preserves

Preheat oven to 350°. Combine dry ingredients, then combine wet ingredients separately. Add wet mixture to dry mixture. Form dough into balls, flatten, indent each circle, and add ½ tsp. of preserves to each center. Bake 15 min. or until edges are golden brown.

Blonde Macaroons (V,GF)

Thanks for the recipe, Stephanie Eastman!

3 C coconut flakes (unsweetened)

1½ C almond flour (grind almonds in VitaMix/Blendtec, but not too long or it turns into almond butter, or use almond flour purchased in a store)

1 C real maple syrup (preferably grade B)

⅓ C melted coconut oil

1 Tbsp. vanilla

½ tsp sea salt

Mix all together well. Form into balls and refrigerate or freeze until firm.

Lemony Bliss Balls (R,V,GF)

Thanks for the recipe, Suzanne!

2 C cashews or almonds, ground

2 C coconut, fresh or dried

¾ C fresh lemon juice

½ C lemon zest

small amount of raw honey or agave, to taste [Use agave for V recipe.]

Blend or process all ingredients to combine. Add extra juice or a little water if needed. The mix should be moist. Form into cookies and dehydrate to taste—but the mix works well simply formed into balls and rolled in coconut. Delish!

Tip: Also works well with lime or orange juice/zest. And passion fruit makes an interesting mix.

Millet Squares (V,GF)

Thanks for the recipe, Tami!

3 C puffed millet cereal
1 C natural peanut or almond butter or NuttZo
¾ C brown rice syrup
4-5 dried apricots, diced
2 Tbsp. goji berries, diced
¼ C pumpkin seeds

Place parchment paper in an 8"x8" pan. Mix dry ingredients in a large bowl. Melt nut butter in a pan with syrup. Pour melted mixture over dry ingredients and mix to coat. Pour into parchment-lined pan and gently press. Place in freezer for about 5 min., until cooled. Remove from pan and cut into desired-sized pieces, then place in a plastic bag and keep in freezer.

Tip: Sometimes the mixture can fall apart into smaller pieces, which are great for topping oatmeal or placing in a bowl with a little almond milk. The Nuttzo adds some good Omega-3s and chia seeds. Yum!!

Raw Fudge (R,V,GF)

Thanks for the recipe, Velda!

¼ C raw honey, raw agave, real maple syrup, or other natural sweetener
1 C coconut oil
½ tsp. vanilla
½ C raw cocoa
¼ C ground walnuts (or nuts of choice)
¼ - ⅓ C hemp hearts

Cream together all ingredients in food processor and press mixture into oiled 8"x8" dish. Sprinkle with coconut, dried cranberries, and/or nuts of choice. Chill. Cut into squares and serve.

Fruit Bars (R,V,GF)

Thanks for the recipe, Vicki Spencer!

- 1½ C pumpkin seeds, ground into a "flour" in blender or food processor
- 2 C grated apple or diced pumpkin or squash
- ½ C sunflower seeds (I soak and dehydrate these before using, but that isn't necessary)
- 1 C dates, apricots, or other dried fruit
- 1 C grated coconut (unsweetened)
- 2 (or more) tsp. cinnamon (I love cinnamon and probably use 2 Tbsp.)

Put all ingredients except the ground pumpkin seeds into food processor and process until smooth. Then add the pumpkin seeds and process until a ball starts to form. Spread mixture on dehydrator trays to desired thickness (I do about ¼"). Dehydrate at 105° for 8+ hours, turning over on the mesh after about 4 hours. Or don't dehydrate—just eat it!

Chips/Crackers

Crispy Corn Chips (R,V,GF)

Thanks for the recipe, Cheryl!

1 large bag frozen corn, thawed completely
1 small red onion, chopped
1 tsp. ground red pepper (or more, to taste)
1 handful fresh cilantro, chopped (or more, to taste)
sea salt, to taste

Blend the first three ingredients together in a food processer until smooth. Hand-stir the cilantro into the mixture. Spread mixture on Para Flex sheets or parchment paper ¼" thick, then sprinkle sea salt over the layer. Dehydrate in dehydrator 3-4 hours. Remove the Para Flex/parchment and flip the chips over. Continue to dehydrate until crispy, about 4-6 hours. When done, break into desired-sized pieces. Chips will crisp up more when left on the counter.

Best "Cheesy" Kale Chips (R,V,GF)

Thanks for the recipe, Corinne!

Chips:

1 bunch organic curly kale, washed, stems removed, torn into bite-sized pieces

Coating:

1 C raw cashews

1 bell pepper (red or yellow), seeded and chopped

¼ C raw apple cider vinegar

juice of 1 lemon

1 tsp. garlic powder

6 Tbsp. nutritional yeast

½ tsp. sea salt

1 large jalapeño

Put all coating ingredients in a blender and blend until smooth. Using your hands, massage coating onto kale pieces, making sure to get it inside of the curls. Put coated kale onto Teflex sheets on dehydrator trays (remove tray above to make room). Dehydrate at 110° for 6 hours. Slide kale chips onto mesh screens and dehydrate another 4 hours or until very crispy. [See Photos section.]

Raw Kale Chips (R,V,GF)

Thanks for the recipe, Jackie King!

Chips:

4-6 bunches kale, washed and then ripped into bite-sized pieces

Coating:

1 C raw tahini

½ C tamari (we substitute brine from our cultured vegetables)

1 C water

½ C nutritional yeast

juice of 2 lemons

4 green onions *OR* ½ regular onion *OR* 1 tsp. onion powder

2 cloves garlic

½ C raw apple cider vinegar

Blend coating ingredients together well, then pour over and massage into kale pieces (especially curls). Dehydrate on 105° until crispy, usually around 24 hours.

Banana-Carrot Flax Crackers (R,V,GF)

Thanks for the recipe, Jo!

1 C golden flax seeds
½ C raw sunflower seeds
¼ C buckwheat
1 qt. filtered water
2 mashed bananas
pulp from about 5 juiced carrots
4 Tbsp raw, organic agave
optional: ¼ C chia seeds

Soak the first four ingredients in the filtered water and let sit 4 hours. Drain excess liquid, if any. You may have to add more water during the soak time if it has all been absorbed early. Then add the bananas, carrot pulp, and agave and mix until well combined. Spread mixture on solid dehydrator sheets about ¼" thick. (I have found that some sheets need a light coating of nonstick spray. I put one little squirt on the tray and spread with my hand.) Dehydrate at 106° until the top is dry, then flip over and finish dehydrating. Drying time varies from 8-12 hours.

Passionate Parsnip Chips (R,V,GF)

Thanks for the recipe, Joyce!

Have a craving for sweet? Root vegetables have a curative effect on sugar imbalances and cravings. Works like a charm every time!

1 lb. parsnips, chopped (and peeled, if you like)
4 Tbsp. extra virgin olive oil
4 oz. water (or more, to desired consistency)
pinch sea salt or manna

Combine all ingredients in a high-powered blender and blend until a mousse consistency. Spread on a teflex and dehydrate for about 6-8 hours.

Variation: Rather than making chips, place the mousse in a bowl and sprinkle with optional 1-2 Tbsp. seeds or chopped nuts (sesame seeds, walnuts, chia seeds, etc.). It's an amazing dip! Scoop away! [See Photos section.]

Tip: You can also try using other root veggies instead, such as celeriac (celery root). This is fast, easy, and versatile recipe!

Flax Crackers (R,V,GF)

Thanks for the recipe, Lezlee!

(Recipe was adapted by Robyn.)

4 C dry flax seeds
¾ lb. (about 3 medium) tomatoes
1 small onion
½ lb. (about 1 C) carrots
½ yellow or red bell pepper
¼ lb. (about 1-2 stalks) celery
2 cloves garlic, minced *OR* 2 tsp. garlic, crushed
1 Tbsp. chili powder (or to taste)
1 tsp. sea salt (or to taste)

Note: Remember that after dehydrating, the flavors will be much more concentrated. Take this into account when deciding how much of the spices to add.

Rinse flax seeds, cover in a large bowl with plenty of water, and soak 4-8 hours. (Flax absorbs several times its own volume of water, so check the bowl occasionally and stir, adding more water if necessary.) Then drain well with a strainer, but do not rinse. Transfer to a bowl.

In a food processor, blend well all other ingredients except chili powder and salt. Add mixture to bowl with flax seeds, add chili powder and salt, and mix together well by hand.

Spread mixture ¼" thick on dehydrator Teflex sheets or, if the mixture is thick enough, on the mesh dehydrator sheets. Dry at 105° for about 15 hours, then turn crackers over and dry another few hours until crispy. Break up into cracker-sized pieces and store in Ziploc bags or containers.

Sorta-Sweet Sunflower-Flaxseed Snack Chips (R,V,GF)

Thanks for the recipe, Sallie!

Soak overnight in 5-6 C spring water:

1 C golden flax seeds

1 C brown flax seeds

1 C sunflower seeds (these will have started to sprout after 10 hrs!)

Soak separately in 1 C spring water:

2 Tbsp. chia seeds (Stir the seeds into the water and continue stirring for a few seconds. After a few minutes, stir again to avoid clumping. Then stir again after 10 min. more. After soaking 30 min., they are totally jelled and ready to use.)

Stir the chia gel into the soaked seed mixture and put into a food processor with an S-blade. Then add any or all of the following ingredients:

½ - 1 C fresh orange or tangerine juice

2-3 Tbsp. almond butter or tahini

½ C hulled hemp seeds

10-20 chopped cacaobonen *OR* ¼ - ½ C cacao nibs

cinnamon, vanilla powder, ginger powder, or maca powder (or any mixture of spices which suit your fancy), to taste

raw agave syrup, raw honey, or real maple syrup, to taste [Use agave or maple syrup for V recipe.]

pinch Celtic or sea salt *OR* if you're adventurous, a nice spoonful of umeboshi plum paste (this is very salty and sour at the same time and gives a nice contrast to the sweetness of the syrups)

Spread the mixture about ⅛" thick onto paraflex sheets and dehydrate on high for 1 hour. (While the food is still wet, the temperature inside the food is much lower than the oven temperature. This cuts the drying time considerably without compromising the quality of the enzymes, as stated by the Excalibur people.) Then turn down to 118° for about 6 hours. When the surface is dry, peel from the sheets, turn over, and continue drying on the sheets.

When dry, cut into squares and store in a Ziploc bag. Enjoy with a clear conscience!

Tip: I usually divide the recipe in half and make two different varieties.

Dips/Spreads

Yogurt Fruit Dip (GF)

Thanks for the recipe, Barbara!

1 C yogurt
1 C coconut milk
2 Tbsp. raw agave
vanilla, to taste

Blend and refrigerate.

Hummus Dip (V,GF)

Thanks for the recipe, Deb!

1 can chickpeas
¼ C lemon
2 medium clove garlic, peeled and crushed
3 Tbsp. tahini
1 Tbsp. extra virgin olive oil
2 Tsp. tamari (natural soy sauce)
pinch chipotle chili powder

Mix all together in a food processer and refrigerate overnight. Use as a dip for your favorite vegetables.

Cinnamon Buzz Spread (R,V,GF)

Thanks for the recipe, Debbie!

¼ C coconut oil
2 Tbsp. raw honey or agave [Use agave for V recipe.]
1 tsp. ground cinnamon

Mix all together well and enjoy!

Raw Onion Dip (R,V,GF)

Thanks for the recipe, Evi from Germany!

A bit expensive, but soooo good!

2 C macadamia nuts
¾ C water (more if needed)
1 C diced yellow onion, marinated in Bragg Liquid Aminos, tamari, or another soy sauce for at least 30 min.

Blend nuts and water in blender or food processor until creamy and thick. Mix in the onions by hand. Chill. Sprinkle Bragg Organic Seasoning on top and enjoy!

Roasted Garlic Hummus (V,GF)

Thanks for the recipe, Evi from Germany!

I like taking this to work with chopped veggies and some whole-grain or flax crackers.

1 large head garlic
2 C cooked (or canned) chickpeas
2 Tbsp. fresh lemon juice
1 Tbsp, tamari or Nama Shoyu
1 Tbsp. tahini (sesame paste)
2 Tbsp. water
2 Tbsp. chopped fresh parsley or chives (what you have on hand)
sea salt to taste
paprika for garnish

Preheat oven to 425°. Remove the loose papery outside skin from the garlic head without separating the cloves. Slice off the top ½" and discard. Wrap garlic in a small square of foil and roast until very soft, about 40 min. (I usually do this when I've got something else in the oven.) Unwrap garlic and cool slightly, then separate the cloves and peel them.

Purée the garlic, chickpeas, lemon juice, tamari, tahini, and water in a food processor. Add more or less water as necessary to make a fairly firm dip. Transfer to a small serving bowl, stir in parsley, and season with salt. Cover and refrigerate for up to 2 days. When ready to serve, garnish with sprig of parsley and sprinkling of paprika.

Sunflower Seed Spread (R,V,GF)

Thanks for the recipe, Evi from Germany!

1 C sunflower seeds
2 C water (or more, depending on desired consistency)
6 Tbsp. milk (rice, coconut, almond, oat, etc.) [Use homemade milk for R recipe.]
1 Tbsp. fresh lemon juice
1 tsp. sea salt

Soak the sunflower seeds in the water overnight. Discard any water that remains. Add milk, lemon juice, and salt, then mix well in a food processor.

This is the basic recipe. You can vary it as you like. Here are some ideas:

- Top with chopped chives, parsley, or other herbs
- Add 1 or 2 garlic cloves when mixing in the food processor
- Top with finely chopped tomatoes and watercress
- Sprinkle on Bragg Liquid Aminos and chopped scallions
- Add finely grated apple
- Add 1 Tbsp. extra virgin olive oil for more of a hummus-like consistency
- Add tomato paste and Italian spices when mixing in the food processor
- Add pineapple and curry when mixing in the food processor

Homemade Sprouted Hummus (R,V,GF)

Thanks for the recipe, James Thomas!

1 lb. garbanzos beans, soaked overnight (see Tip below)
4 Tbsp. raw tahini (sesame paste)
½ lemon
1 Tbsp. raw apple cider vinegar
5 cloves garlic
1" piece fresh ginger
½ tsp. cayenne
½ tsp. curry
2 Tbsp. miso
6 pods cardamom seed
1 tsp. cumin
1 star anise
1 tsp. fennel
5 green peppercorns
1 Tbsp. coriander seeds
water (up to ½ C) for thick and creamy consistency

Place all ingredients into blender and blend until smooth. Refrigerate. Smother hummus on a bed of kale leaves or make wraps. Garnish hummus with flower petals: calendulas, lavender, marigolds, etc. Sprinkle on some fresh hemp. Use your intuition! Be flexible!

Tip: I usually soak three pounds of garbanzo beans for 24 hours until they sprout. Then I freeze leftover beans in a Ziploc bag for another use.

Superfast Hot Pink Veggie Dip (GF)

Thanks for the recipe, Janie!

2 Tbsp. finely diced shallots or onions
1-1½ C finely diced carrots
1 beet, diced into small pieces
7 oz. cream cheese
2 tsp. Madras curry powder (buy or make your own)
½ tsp. sea salt
optional: 1 handful fresh wild mushrooms

Hand mix all ingredients until well combined, then mix in Thermomix or high-powered blender for 30 sec. *Serves 4-6 for lunch or 8-10 as a dip.*

Cinnamon-Vanilla Pecan Butter (R,V,GF)

Thanks for the recipe, Kandace!

10 oz. pecans
½ Tbsp. pure vanilla extract
½ Tbsp. ground cinnamon
⅛ tsp. sea salt
½ tsp. coconut oil

Blend all the ingredients in a food processor or high-powered blender. [See Photos section.]

Vanilla Butter Apple Dip (V,GF)

Thanks for the recipe, Kaysie Campbell!

Can be a snack or light meal.

¼ C any nut butter (my favorite are peanut butter and sunflower seed butter)
¼ C vanilla coconut milk yogurt
optional: vanilla brown rice protein powder (Jay Robb or Sun Warrior brand) [Use vegan powder for V recipe.]

Mix all ingredients until homogenized and use for an apple dip. *Makes enough to eat with 1 apple cut into very thin slices.* [See Photos section.]

Almond Paté (R,V,GF)

Thanks for the recipe, Larissa!

1½ C sprouted almonds
1 Tbsp. fresh (or 1-2 tsp. powdered) ginger
1 clove fresh (or 1 tsp. powdered) garlic
juice of 2 lemons
pinch sea salt

Mix all in blender until fully blended. Add water as needed to help blend. It should be a bit thicker than hummus. It will stay good in fridge for 2-3 days. Great as a veggie dip or a spread. And I even use this in my vegan raw sushi, and my husband uses it on chicken before baking it! It's amazing.

Paté (R,V)

Thanks for the recipe, Lezlee!

(Recipe was adapted by Robyn.)

2 C raw almonds, soaked overnight
½ white onion, chopped
½ C fresh parsley, chopped
2 cloves garlic
¼ C fresh lemon juice
¼ C flaxseed oil
1 tsp. Vege-Sal (salt replacement) or sea salt

In a food processor, blend all ingredients into a paste. Use as a dip or a filling/spread.

> ***Tip:*** You can add Mexican, Italian, Asian, French, vegetable, etc., seasonings to make this paté very different.

Creamy Veggie Dip for Artichokes (GF)

Thanks for the recipe, Lisa Fielding!

2 handfuls spinach
1 handful kale
4-5 cloves garlic
¼ C extra virgin olive oil
1 squirt mustard
1 tsp. dry mustard
sea salt and pepper, to taste
Romano cheese, to taste (about ¼ - ½ C)
¼ C pepperoncini brine or balsamic vinegar
chia seeds, to thicken and gel (about 3 Tbsp.)
1 bunch cilantro *OR* ½ C fresh basil (best)
vegetable broth or water, to achieve desired thickness
optional: 2 Tbsp. Vegannaise

Blend all in blender well, chill, and serve. Great as an artichoke or bread dip, drizzled over steamed asparagus, added to chicken or fish, stirred into rice before or after cooking. Can be frozen in 1 C portions for future use.

Sunflower Fall Paté (R,V,GF)

Thanks for the recipe, Mimi!

What I love about this paté is that it can be sweet or savory depending on what it's served with. I've had it in collard wraps for lunch and on top of sprouted toast for breakfast.

1 C soaked sunflower seeds
½ C zucchini
½ C shredded or diced carrot
¾ C fresh cranberries, divided (dried works too, but I like fresh)
sprinkling of diced onion
½ tsp. salt
½ tsp. cinnamon
1 tsp. dried rosemary
thyme, to taste
nutmeg and cloves, to taste
1 Tbsp. apple cider or balsamic vinegar
1½ Tbsp. real maple syrup or sweetener of choice [Use maple syrup for V,GF recipe; use raw honey for R,GF recipe; use raw agave for R,V,GF recipe.]
optional: pinch stevia

Blend sunflower seeds with the veggies and half the cranberries, then add in the spices and liquids. (You might want to add a little bit of water to get things moving.) Adjust seasonings to taste. Toss in the other half of the cranberries and process just enough to incorporate.

Munchies

Sweet Corn (V,GF)

Thanks for the recipe, Cindy!

2 Tbsp. coconut oil
½ C unpopped popcorn kernels
3 Tbsp. Xylitol
1 tsp. sea salt

In a large pan (that has a lid), heat the coconut oil uncovered on medium heat. When oil is hot enough (test by carefully placing 1 kernel in pan—if it pops, oil is ready; remove popped kernal after testing), add the rest of the ingredients to the pan and put the lid on. Gently shake the pan back and forth while still on the burner. This keeps the kernels and popcorn from burning. As the popcorn pops, continue to shake it so the unpopped kernels fall to the bottom and pop. Once popping completely stops, immediately remove from heat and pour into a bowl. Let cool for a few minutes as the Xyletol will be especially hot and will burn you.

Note: This recipe will work only with Xylitol. Substituting a different sweetener will cause it to turn dark and burn.

Crunchy Chickpeas (V,GF)

Thanks for the recipe, Evi!

1 can chickpeas (or cook them yourself)
1Tbsp. extra virgin olive oil
1 Tbsp. sea salt or Original Crystal Himalayan Salt
2 tsp. spice mixture, your choice (e.g., garam masala, curry, chili, garlic powder, etc.)

Preheat oven to 400°. Drain chickpeas, then rinse, drain well, and pat dry. Place chickpeas and olive oil in a Ziploc bag and shake well until the oil is evenly distributed. Place oiled chickpeas on a baking sheet (I also use baking paper) and roast for 30-45 min. Jiggle the chickpeas every 10 min. or so, to prevent burning. You need to watch them closely and remove from oven only when they are truly crispy. Place chickpeas in a bowl, add salt and spices, and mix well.

Sweet Candied Nuts (GF)

Thanks for the recipe, Jennette!

16 C raw nuts (almonds, walnuts, pecans, cashews, or a mixture)
⅔ C pure maple syrup
1½ tsp. pure vanilla extract
2 Tbsp. cinnamon
½ tsp. nutmeg
½ Tbsp. sea salt
1½ C Sucanat

Soak the nuts for 6-8 hours, drain, and then dehydrate at 105° for approximately 24 hours (until crunchy). Transfer nuts to a large bowl and coat with maple syrup and vanilla, then let sit. Combine all the dry ingredients (salt, cinnamon, nutmeg, and Sucanat) in a separate bowl, and then sprinkle over nuts while mixing. Return nuts to the dehydrator for another 12-24 hours. [See Photos section.]

Maple-Sugared Nuts (GF)

Thanks for the recipe, Kathy!

⅓ C real maple syrup
⅛ tsp. salt
2 C raw almonds, pecans, or walnuts

Heat skillet over medium-high heat until hot. Turn heat down to medium and pour in maple syrup and salt. Immediately pour in nuts and stir to coat evenly with syrup. Continue to cook stirring constantly for 3 min. (Almonds will take about 5 min. longer—if they are still sticky, cook a bit longer.)

Place nuts on cutting board to cool. Great as a snack or tossed into a salad!

Pumpkin Seed Brittle (R,V,GF)

Thanks for the recipe, Madi!

1 lb. raw pumpkin seeds
4 Tbsp. raw, organic agave
⅓ tsp. cayenne
⅓ tsp. paprika
⅓ tsp. chili powder

Mix all together and dehydrate to crisp.

Hansel and Gretel Mix (R,V,GF)

Thanks for the recipe, Robyn (not GreenSmoothieGirl—a different Robyn)!

1 C goji berries
1 C cacao nibs
1 C raw sunflower seeds
1 C raw pumpkin seeds

Mix everything together in a bowl. This recipe has infinite variations. Add hemp seeds, sesame seeds, crushed nuts, dried currants, raisins, sultanas, dried apricot/pineapple/ mango chunks, etc. For extra enzyme action, soak the nuts overnight, rinse, and dehydrate until dried out. For mega nutrients, sprout the seeds before deyhdrating. [See Photos section.]

"Cheesy" Chickpeas (V,GF)

Thanks for the recipe, Stephanie (adapted from Vegan Lunch Box by Jennifer McCann)!

(Recipe was adapted by Robyn.)

1 can chickpeas/garbanzo beans, rinsed & drained *OR* 1½ C cooked or sprouted chickpeas, drained
1 Tbsp. extra virgin olive oil
2 tsp. Brewer's or nutritional yeast flakes
½ tsp. Original Crystal Himalayan Salt

Toss chickpeas with olive oil, yeast flakes, and salt. Eat immediately, dry until crunchy in the dehydrator below 115°, or store in refrigerator. Or for a great hot, crunchy snack, spread the mixture on a cookie sheet lined with parchment paper and roast in a 400° oven for about 30 min. [See Photos section.]

Movie Night Popcorn (V,GF)

Thanks for the recipe, Tara!

8 C (or more) air-popped popcorn
½ C coconut oil, melted
1 Tbsp. nutritional yeast
2 tsp. curry powder
dash Spirulina powder
sea salt, to taste
Zesty salt-free blend (from San Francisco Herb Company), to taste

Mix coconut oil with popcorn, tossing to coat. Separately mix together remaining dry ingredients and sprinkle on popcorn, to taste.

Smoothies & Other Drinks

Smoothies

Morning Berry Bliss (GF)

Thanks for the recipe, Amanda!

⅓ C whole milk organic yogurt
⅓ C coconut, almond, or rice milk*
1 Tbsp. flaxseed oil
1 scoop Sun Warrior protein powder (vanilla or natural flavor)
1 C packed organic spinach
1 C frozen mixed berries

**Fruit juice (orange, cranberry, açaí, etc.) is also delicious instead of milk. Make sure it's 100% fruit juice, not from concentrate.*

Blend all ingredients together except for the frozen mixed berries and mix well. After everything is well incorporated, add the mixed berries and blend a little bit more.

Red Vegetable Smoothie (R,V,GF)

Thanks for the recipe, Amanda!

1 C apple juice (organic, unsweetened)
½ cucumber, peeled
1 celery stalk, cut into 3" pieces
1½ C carrots
¼ radish
1 apple, cored and cut into eighths
½ Tbsp. dried parsley
¼ C ice

Blend all in blender until smooth.

Cool Cucumber Delight (R,V,GF)

Thanks for the recipe, Amy!

1 cucumber with peel
1 C water
1 ripe banana
1 apple, cut into 4 pieces (with seeds, skin, and stem included)
5 chard leaves (any variety)
1 handful ice

Blend it all together for 30 seconds and enjoy!

Alien Juice (R,V,GF)

Thanks for the recipe, Angela!

2 handfuls baby bok choy
2 handfuls organic spinach
1 pear
½ avocado
1 tsp. chia seeds
½ tsp. kelp
1½ C mixed fruit (Costco: mango, strawberry, and pineapple frozen mix)
1 C rice milk [Use homemade milk for R recipe.]

Blend until smooth.

Yummy Fruit Smoothie (GF)

Thanks for the recipe, Angie!

1 C almond milk
few handfuls spinach
fresh strawberries and blueberries, to fill blender
1 Tbsp. flax seeds
1 small container plain yogurt
½ tsp. vanilla
1 packet stevia
1-2 bananas

Blend up and enjoy! You can also substitute dandelion or any other availabe green for spinach.

A Taste of Mexico (R,V,GF)

Thanks for the recipe, Ann!

16 oz. cold distilled water
1 celery stalk (about ½ C)
1 handful spinach and romaine
little bit of parsley and cilantro
1 clove garlic
½ lime or lemon
optional: ½ ripe avocado (if you want it thick)

Blend in high-powered blender. Delicious for lunch or dinner!

Ann's Fabulous Fruit Drink (R,V,GF)

Thanks for the recipe, Ann!

2 C apple
1 C grapes
1 C blackberries
4-5 rose hips
¼ C sprouts
⅛ C flax meal
3 C grape juice

Blend all ingredients in blender. I substitute whatever fruits are in season.

Pineapple Raspberry Smoothie (R,V,GF)

Thanks for the recipe, Annette!

4 C spinach
½ fresh pineapple (including core)
1 C fresh raspberries
1 C ice

Blend away!

Cruciferous Cancer Kicker (R,V,GF)

Thanks for the recipe, Aubrey!

1-2 C cauliflower
1 young coconut (meat and water)
spirulina and/or chlorella

Blend until smooth. Enjoy!!

Betsy's "Can't Live Without It" Green Drink (R,V,GF)

Thanks for the recipe, Betsy!

2-2½ C water
1 Tbsp. hemp seeds
1 Tbsp. flax seeds
½ banana
1 organic apple *OR* 1 organic pear
5-7 C organic greens (kale, spinach, and/or arugula; I usually do a combination of 2 greens)
6-7 oz. frozen organic berries (any kind)

Blend in high-powered blender until smooth.

Good Green Morning (R,V,GF)

Thanks for the recipe, Bev!

(Recipe was adapted by Robyn.)

2 oranges
1 apple
½ banana
1 C strawberries (fresh or frozen)
lots of greens

Blend all in blender until smooth. Can vary the strawberries with pineapple, peaches, mango, blueberries, etc., but the basic oranges, apple, and banana stays the same.

Upside-Down Monkey Smoothie (R,V,GF)

Thanks for the recipe, Bill!

½ fresh papaya
1 apple
1 banana
1 C apple juice (organic, unsweetened)
5-6 ice cubes
optional: 3 dates, pitted

Blend all together. Yummy!

Strawberry Lemonade Green Smoothie (R,V,GF)

Thanks for the recipe, Billy!

10 frozen strawberries
⅛ - ¼ lemon with peel *OR* ½ lemon without peel
2 large handfuls spinach or other greens (you can always add more greens)
1 Tbsp. raw agave nectar or stevia, to taste
¼ C chia gel (made by soaking 2 tsp. chia seeds in scant ¼ C water for 1 hour)

Blend all ingredients, serve, and enjoy!

Note: I find that lemon really helps with flavor when I am trying to decrease the fruit I am using. I have also used lime (and lime peel) as well with great results.

Blake's Fresh Flax Seed Smoothie (GF)

Thanks for the recipe, Blake!

3-4 oz. frozen pineapple or mango
1 banana
½ C plain yogurt (I like Seven Stars)
½ C almond milk
2-4 Tbsp. fresh ground flax seeds (I grind them myself every morning)

Place all ingredients into blender and mix.

Super Green Power Smoothie (R,V,GF)

Thanks for the recipe, Bob!

½ avocado
3 C spinach
1 C peas
juice of ½ lime
½ garlic clove
1½ tsp. curry power
½ - ⅓ C water

Blend all in blender until desired thickness.

Chard Strawbana Smoothie (R,V,GF)

Thanks for the recipe, Brooke!

2 C water
2 Tbsp. flax seeds
2 Tbsp. pumpkin seeds
2 Medjool dates
4-6 Swiss chard leaves or equivalent volume of beet greens (or combo of both)
spinach added to make 4 C
2 bananas
14 frozen strawberries

Soak the flax seeds, pumpkin seeds, and dates in the water for about 10 min. Blend water, seeds, dates, and chard/beet greens. Then add spinach until blended volume is 4 C. Add bananas and frozen strawberries and blend until smooth. *Makes 1½ qt.*

Fruity Green Smoothie (R,V,GF)

Thanks for the recipe, Candis!

2 C water
1 kale leaf, with stalk
1 handful sprouts
1 cabbage leaf
2 handfuls spinach
1 banana
1 pear
1 small apple
2 handfuls cherries

Put all ingredients into blender and blend to desired consistency.

Breakfast Fruit Smoothie (R,V,GF)

Thanks for the recipe, Carolyn!

12 (or so) almonds
½ C water if fruit is frozen *OR* 1 C crushed ice if fruit is fresh
1 banana
½ C pineapple (fresh is preferred)
1- 1½ C your favorite fruit or fruit combo
2 Tbsp. protein powder [Use vegan, raw powder for V,R recipe.]
1 tsp. greens powder *OR* ½ C alfalfa sprouts

Use Smoothie setting on Blendtec and blend almonds and water first until smooth. Then add remaining ingredients and blend again until smooth.

Cele's Favorite Green Smoothie (R,V,GF)

Thanks for the recipe, Cecilia!

8 kale leaves
2 handfuls spinach
1 grapefruit
3 celery stalks
4 medium green apples
1 frozen banana
1 frozen mango
1 heaping tsp. ground flax seeds

First juice the first five ingredients. Then transfer to a blender and add the rest of the ingredients. Blend until very smooth. Delicious!

Grapefruit Sunrise (R,V,GF)

Thanks for the recipe, Cendrine!

juice of 2 grapefruit*
juice of 4 oranges*
1 C strawberries (fresh or frozen)
2 tsp. raw honey or raw agave [Use agave for V recipe.]
sections from 1 grapefruit
½ C sliced strawberries

**Chill the fruit first for cold juice, or add some ice cubes while blending.*

Place grapefruit juice, orange juice, 1 C strawberries, and honey in blender and blend until smooth. Strain into two chilled glasses. Top with grapefruit sections and sliced strawberries. *Serves 2.* [See Photos section.]

Note: One serving of this drink provides 411% of the Daily Value (DV) for vitamin C, 26% DV for potassium, and 26% DV for folate.

Peach-Mango Tango (R,V,GF)

Thanks for the recipe, Cheryl!

1 mango, diced
¼ C Craisins (soaked)
1 C tangerine or orange juice
1 peach, diced
2 C spinach or kale

Blend until smooth. Enjoy!

Watermelon Smoothie (R,V,GF)

Thanks for the recipe, Cheryl!

½ "personal size" watermelon
1-2 handfuls any greens you like (organic baby spinach, dandelion, kale, collard greens, etc.)
optional: 1 packet stevia (if you need a little sweetener)

Blend it all up in the blender. Yum!

"To Your Health" Green Juice (R,V,GF)

Thanks for the recipe, Christine!

1 large bunch kale
1 small bok choy
4 celery stalks
4 Napa cabbage leaves
1 cucumber
2 handfuls spinach
2 Granny Smith apples
1 "thumb" ginger
2 large carrots

Combine all ingredients and blend well.

Lime-Kissed Powerhouse (R,V,GF)

Thanks for the recipe, Cindy Chandler (www.SmoothScentSations.com)!

8 oz. water
1 Tbsp. blackstrap molasses
2 strawberries
¼ orange, peeled
1/6 lime (including peel)
15 almonds
1 carrot
2 C spinach or kale
½ banana
2 Tbsp. flax seeds
1 Tbsp. nutritional yeast
1 C ice
optional: Ormus Greens, for an extra boost

Mix all in high-powered blender.

Coral's Quick Fruit Smoothie (R,V,GF)

Thanks for the recipe, Coral!

2 C water
1 Tbsp. flax seeds
1 apple, cut into chunks
1 orange, peeled and sectioned
1 banana
optional: ice

In a blender, first blend water and flax seeds. Then add the fruit in one at a time while continuing to blend.

Berry Bliss Smoothie (R,V,GF)

Thanks for the recipe, Courtney!

3 celery stalks
1 apple
1 fresh banana
½ C frozen mango
1 C frozen berry mix
1 C coconut water

Blend until smooth. Delicious and decadent. Enjoy!

Dirty Greens (R,V,GF)

Thanks for the recipe, Damien!

1-2 handfuls spinach
2 small bananas (or 1 large)
water from 1 young coconut
1 Tbsp. flaxseed oil or coconut oil
1-1½ Tbsp. cacao powder
1 tsp. - 1 Tbsp. spirulina powder
tiny pinch stevia powder
optional: 1 tsp. - 1 Tbsp. bee pollen
optional: pinch lightly soaked goji berries

Combine all ingredients in a blender and mix well.

Mineral Power Smoothie (R,V,GF)

Thanks for the recipe, Dan!

This makes an incredibly nutritious drink that will fill a large glass, provide enough for pouring over granola for breakfast, and fill a glass jar for use throughout the day and/or the next day. Some may like to cut back on the fruit and enjoy the bitter taste of minerals, which kale is so full of.

- 5½ C ionized filtered (alkaline) water
- 1 bunch kale (including stalks)
- 2 apples, thinly sliced
- 2 bananas
- ¼ "- ½" thick slice pineapple, depending on size
- 4 Tbsp. hemp hearts (shelled hemp seeds)

Liquefy the kale in the water first, then add the rest of the ingredients and blend again.

Creamy Sunny Berry Smoothie (R,V,GF)

Thanks for the recipe, Dawn!

- 1 large handful spinach (or collard greens, chard, etc.—or some of each)
- 2 kale stalks, with largest part of stalk on the end removed
- 1 apple or pear (fresh or frozen)
- 1 peach or mango (fresh or frozen)
- 1-2 bananas (fresh or frozen)
- several large spoonfuls frozen blueberries (or other berries)
- 1 C fresh pineapple juice (or other juice)
- 1 C creamy coconut milk (1 C hot water + 1 C dry shredded coconut)
- 2 tsp. fresh lemon juice
- 1 squirt liquid stevia *OR* 1 spoonful dry stevia
- sesame seeds (calcium), flax seeds (omegas), almonds (good protein/fat), etc. (as much as desired)

Combine and blend for 1-2 min. Strain pulp and serve.

Tip: Use pulp in cookies, muffins, or other smoothies.

Sunny Berry Smoothie (R,V,GF)

Thanks for the recipe, Dawn!

1 large handful spinach (or collard greens, chard, or some of each)
2 kale stalks, with largest part of stalk on the end removed
1 apple or pear (fresh or frozen)
1-2 banana (fresh or frozen)
1 peach, mango, nectarine, or other fruit (fresh or frozen)
several large spoonfuls frozen blueberries (or other berries)
1 C fresh pineapple juice (or other juice)
1 Tbsp. fresh lemon juice
1 squirt liquid stevia *OR* 1 spoonful dry stevia
sesame seeds (calcium), flax seeds (omegas), almonds (good protein/fat), etc.

Blend baby blend!

Cinful Peach (R,V,GF)

Thanks for the recipe, Deb!

1 frozen banana, chunked
½ C frozen sliced peaches
1 apple *OR* 1 pear
¾ - 1 C fresh orange juice
1-2 shakes cinnamon
2-3 handfuls kale
1 Tbsp. raw blue agave syrup

Hit the Smoothie button on your Blendtec and…heaven!

Cherry Delight (R,V,GF)

Thanks for the recipe, Deb (deb-toyourhealth.blogspot.com)!

2 C filtered water
2 bananas
1 big handful frozen cherries
2 kale leaves *OR* 2 handfuls spinach

Blend all ingredients in high-powered blender until it is a creamy smoothie and enjo—some for now and some for later! (Or share it with the kiddos!)

Chocolate Smoothie Too (R,V,GF)

Thanks for the recipe, Deb G.!

2 young coconuts (water and meat)
¼ C hemp
1 scoop protein powder (chocolate or vanilla)
1 heaping Tbsp. cacao powder
1 Tbsp. carob powder
4 dates
2 frozen bananas
optional: 1 handful goji berries

Blend and enjoy!

Chocolate Strawberry Delight (R,V,GF)

Thanks for the recipe, Debra!

1 avocado
1 Tbsp. cocoa (non-alkalized)
1 tsp. stevia
8 strawberries

Mix well in your blender. Optionally slice more strawberries for on top.

Summer Sour (R,V,GF)

Thanks for the recipe, Debra!

1 (6 oz.) bag spinach
1 apple
1 banana
1 whole lemon
1 C frozen pineapple
2 C water

Blend in blender and enjoy.

Greener Sunshine Joy (R,V,GF)

Thanks for the recipe, Dede!

1½ C freshly cut pineapple
8-10 large kale leaves (preferably Lacinato)
3-4 pitted & non-sulphured dates *OR* stevia, to desired sweetness
1 C alfalfa sprouts
15-20 spearmint leaves
ice

Blend everything together to desired consistency. I hope you love this as much as I do!

Date-Banana Shake (R,V,GF)

Thanks for the recipe, Delia!

2 C almond milk
6-8 dates
2 frozen bananas
18-20 ice cubes
1 tsp. vanilla

Blend ingredients together in a high-powered blender until smooth and enjoy.

Watch Your Weight Smoothie (V,GF)

Thanks for the recipe, Denise!

1 scoop protein powder
1½ C pure coconut water
½ C raw kefir liquid
2 C baby spinach (raw, organic)
1 rounded tsp. Tocotrienols
1 tsp. organic coconut milk powder
1 frozen banana
3-4 ice cubes

Blend all ingredients until smooth.

Avocado-Banana-Hemp-Berry Smoothie (R,V,GF)

Thanks for the recipe, Dennis!

½ ripe avocado
1-1½ frozen bananas
4-5 strawberries (fresh or frozen)
¼ - ½ C almond milk
1 Tbsp. hemp protein powder
1 Tbsp. hulled hemp seeds
pinch cinnamon
optional: 1-2 Tbsp. hemp oil

Add all ingredients into a blender and mix well.

Tip: I buy the hemp products at www.hempoilcan.com.

Popeye's Passion (R,V,GF)

Thanks for the recipe, Diana (www.DianaStobo.com)!

2 C fresh-pressed apple juice (or organic, unsweetened)
2 C fresh organic spinach
1 frozen banana

Place all ingredients in blender and blend on high for 30-40 sec. until creamy. Enjoy immediately! *Makes 1 serving.*

Sugar Beet Smoothie (R,V,GF)

Thanks for the recipe, Elizabete!

1 collard green leaf
½ small sugar beet
2 Tbsp. açaí berries or juice
1 C fresh orange juice
1-2 Tbsp. flax seeds
2 bananas

Blend all in blender. It's yummy and healthy!

Alegria Smoothie (R,V,GF)

Thanks for the recipe, Eunice!

1 banana
1 mango
1 guava
1 pear
1 bunch kale
1 bunch spinach
1 bunch collard green
1 bunch watercress
1 bunch alfalfa
1 celery stick
ginger, to taste
¼ lemon
3 Tbsp. spirulina
1 Tbsp. sesame seeds
1 Tsp. bee pollen
1 Tbsp. açaí
1 Tbsp. flaxseed oil
2 Tbsp. agave

Blend all until smooth and enjoy!

Chocolate Smoothie (R,V,GF)

Thanks for the recipe, Findabair!

1 banana (fresh or frozen)
4 strawberries (fresh or frozen)
1 handful black currants (fresh or frozen)
1 tsp. raw carob powder
1 heaping tsp. raw cacao
pinch sea salt
1 tsp. vanilla essence
1 C water (or more, if you like it thinner)
optional: grapes are good here too
optional: 1 tsp. raw honey
optional: super foods like mesquite, maca, blue corn extract, etc.

Blend all together and enjoy!

Yolk Lover's Smoothie (R,V,GF)

Thanks for the recipe, Gene!

1 orange, peeled

1-2 Golden Delicious apples, cored and sliced

2-3 baby carrots

1 Tbsp. raw, organic agave

mixed frozen fruit: strawberries, mangos, pineapples, and peaches (I use Dole brand mix and add extra strawberries)

1 scoop protein/green food mix

4 oz. water (or more, as needed)

4 large ice cubes

Blend on high, adding water and ice to 32 oz. Enjoy!

Graceful Green Smoothie (R,V,GF)

Thanks for the recipe, Grace!

1 C water

6 frozen strawberries

1 apple, cut up

greens, to the top of the blender (alternate kale and spinach)

Blend unitl smooth. It is amazing.

Wheatgrass-Mango Smoothie (R,V)

Thanks for the recipe, Holly!

½ blender full fresh wheatgrass

2 ripe bananas

1 C frozen mangos

water, enough to blend

Because wheatgrass is so fibrous I do this in two steps. First, blend wheatgrass with some water for a few seconds. Then add bananas and mangos and maybe a splash more water. Blend until smooth.

Mateo's Treat (R,V,GF)

Thanks for the recipe, Ingrid!

1 raw mango, cut into small pieces
1 large cucumber, cut into pieces
1 C cold water
optional: stevia to sweeten, to taste

Blend all ingredients in a blender.

Berry-Coconut Smoothie (R,V)

Thanks for the recipe, Jamie!

1 C almond milk or coconut water
1 C spinach or another dark leafy green
½ handful wheat grass
optional: ½ C frozen berries
optional: coconut flakes to taste, flaxseed

Pulse a few times to incorporate. Then blend until smooth and drink up! Delicious!

Banana-Almond Smoothie (R,V,GF)

Thanks for the recipe, Janna!

1 C almond milk
1½ - 2 C baby spinach
½ - ¾ frozen banana
1-2 dates, preferably soaked overnight
few drops pure almond extract (organic, if you can find it)
3-5 ice cubes
optional: few orange sections

Blend almond milk and spinach together well. Then add the rest of the ingredients to the blender and blend again.

Healthy Yummy Fruity Smoothie (R,V,GF)

Thanks for the recipe, Jenni!

1 Tbsp. chia seeds (soaked 15 min.)
1 scoop raw Sun Warrior protein powder
1 C mixed berries
1 green apple
1 Tbsp. spirulina

Blend all together. Thick, healthy, and amazing.

Breakfast Blast Smoothie (GF)

Thanks for the recipe, Jennifer!

½ C frozen organic blueberries
¼ C frozen organic raspberries or cherries
½ C plain, unsweetened yogurt
1 Tbsp. flax seeds
1 Tbsp. chia seeds
1 shake cinnamon
1 scoop vanilla protein powder (SunWarrior or Jay Robb)
2 oz. organic cherry juice (or I may also use Pom or Açaí)
6 oz. water
ice
optional: ¾ C packed spinach

Blend all together until the consistency is right for you. This is like taking a multivitamin every morning—so good for you!

"The Julius" Green Smoothie (R,V,GF)

Thanks for the recipe, Jessica!

Delicious and reminiscent of an Orange Julius smoothie from the mall—and truly hits the spot when feeling a bit under the weather.

1 banana
2 large oranges, peeled
2-3 C packed spinach
1 handful parsley
2 tsp. vanilla extract (or water from soaked vanilla bean)
5 ice cubes
12 oz. water
optional: 1 Tbsp. raw, organic agave

Blend all and enjoy!

Jim's Fruit Smoothie (R,V,GF)

Thanks for the recipe, Jim!

½ C almond milk
1 medium apple
½ avocado
1 banana
½ C frozen blueberries
½ tsp. cinnamon
1 tsp. ginger
1 C grapes
½ C mixed berries
1 C pineapple
1 tsp. rosemary
½ tsp. sage
2 frozen strawberries

Add all to blender and mix thoroughly.

Jim's Vegetable Smoothie (R,V,GF)

Thanks for the recipe, Jim!

½ C alfalfa sprouts
½ medium bell pepper, any color
1 C carrots
4 springs fresh cilantro
½ tsp. cinnamon
½ C collard greens
¼ C dandelion greens
2 Tbsp. flax seeds
1 clove garlic
1 tsp. ginger
52 drops green tea extract
1 C green beans
½ C kale
1 tsp. maca powder
5 fresh mushrooms
3 sprigs fresh parsley
1 tsp. rosemary
½ tsp. sage
1 C spinach
5 frozen strawberries
1 medium tomato
½ tsp. turmeric

Combine all ingredients in blender and mix thoroughly.

Plum Good (R,V,GF)

Thanks for the recipe, Jim!

2 ripe bananas
2 ripe plums
2 oranges, with as much of the white pith as you can keep
3 C filtered water
5-6 bok choy stalks
2-3 C spinach
4-5 large collard green leaves
1 handful cranberries (I use frozen)
1 C açaí berry juice
1½ C green grapes
1 apple

Blend together until smooth. Add a little ice if you like it colder, then blend a little more. *Makes 4 qt.*

Berry-Greens Smoothie (R,V,GF)

Thanks for the recipe, Joanna!

This striking purple smoothie is as delicious as it is beautiful. Use just spinach (no collards) for people who are new to green smoothies and then sit back as they start raving about it and the fact that "you can't taste it has spinach in it!"

2 C strawberries
1 C blueberries
1 C frozen cherries
2 bananas
several collard leaves
1 large handful spinach

Blend all until smooth.

Lemon-Pepper Tomato Greenie (GF)

Thanks for the recipe, John!

½ C filtered water
¼ C plain, non-fat yogurt
¼ tsp. vanilla
1½ C spinach
1 C kale (just leafy part, no stems)
2 Roma tomatoes
2 Tbsp. non-salt lemon pepper (I've had really good results with Mrs. Dash)
frozen or fresh fruit, any kind or amount
optional: raw, organic agave syrup, to sweeten
optional: 1 scoop your favorite protein powder, esp. after a workout (chocolate is my fave)

Blend all until smooth.

Pumpkin Berry Bliss (V,GF)

Thanks for the recipe, Jolene!

2 handfuls raw spinach
1 apple
½ C pumpkin
1 C triple-berry mix (frozen)
water, to blend

Blend thoroughly in high-powered blender. [See Photos section.]

Minty Blue Smoothie (R,V,GF)

Thanks for the recipe, Judy!

2 C blueberries
1 handful (or more) fresh mint
water to thin

Blend all in blender. Enjoy!

Grape-Coconut Smoothie (V,GF)

Thanks for the recipe, Julie!

1 C green grapes
1 C baby spinach or kale (or a mix)
½ C ice
¼ C coconut milk (unsweetened)

Put all in blender *in order listed*, blend, enjoy—and get ready to make more! [See Photos section.]

Justin's Atomic Super Smoothie (R,V,GF)

Thanks for the recipe, Justin!

3 C water or kefir
2 Tbsp. Brewers or nutritional yeast
2 Tbsp. chia seeds
2 Tbsp. goji berries
2 Tbsp. cacao nibs
2 Tbsp. pumpkin seeds
1 Tbsp. spirulina (NOW Brand - Hawaiian)
30 raw almonds
½ whole lemon, cut into small pieces
2 heaping handfuls spinach
3 C different fruits (1 C each type)
cinnamon, to taste

Add everything to the blender and mix. May need to thin with additional water. *Makes 3 full quarts.*

Banana-Berry Smoothie (R,V,GF)

Thanks for the recipe, Karen!

1 banana
1-1½ C berries (I combine raspberries, blackberries, strawberries)
1 C pineapple
1 large handful spinach
¼ C brown sesame seeds
1 Tbsp. flax seeds
⅛ C sunflower seeds
¼ tsp. licorice root
water (to desired consistency)

Put all in blender and blend until smooth.

Morning Smoothie (R,V,GF)

Thanks for the recipe, Karen!

1 large handful baby spinach
2 large leeks *OR* 2 large collard or kale leaves
2 Tbsp. flax seeds
1 banana
1 carrot
1-2 C berries (fresh or frozen)
1 pear or apple
1 C water

Mix in a high-powered blender and serve. *Makes enough for 2 people.*

Sunnyside Up Smoothie (R,V,GF)

Thanks for the recipe, Karen!

I love the flavor, and the seeds all add proteins and nutrients that we need.

1 banana
1 handful raspberries, blackberries, and strawberries combined
½ -1 C fresh pineapple
¼ C sesame seeds
1 Tbsp. flax seeds
⅛ C sunflower seeds
water, to desired consistency

Put all ingredients into a blender and add enough water to make it your desired consistency, then blend until smooth.

Drinkable Supplements (V,GF)

Thanks for the recipe, Kari!

1 Tbsp. Brewer's yeast (for vitamin B)
1 Tbsp. lecithin (GMO free, for healthy blood)
1 Tbsp. ground flax seeds (for Omega-3 oils)
1 Tbsp. ground chia seeds (for ancient proteins)
1 lemon, lime, or orange (for vitamin C)
1 banana, apple, or carrot (to hold it all together)
3 handfuls your favorite greens (for all of us green drink lovers!)
raw blue agave syrup or raw honey, to taste
water, to make it the consistency you like

Blend together and enjoy!

Berry Beginner (GF)

Thanks for the recipe, Kathee!

½ C 100% fruit juice (Very Berry brand is my favorite)
1 C frozen mixed berries
½ banana
2 C organic baby spinach or mixed spring greens
optional: 2 Tbsp. plain nonfat yogurt
optional: 1 C crushed ice

Blend in blender until smooth.

Kicked-Up Smoothie (R,V,GF)

Thanks for the recipe, Katherine!

The blend of sweetness from the watermelon with the green of the spinach and the kick from cayenne is so refreshing!

2 handfuls spinach
4 C watermelon
½ - 1 tsp. cayenne (depending on heat units of the cayenne)
water, to desired consistency

Mix in blender, adding just enough water to get to the desired consistency.

My First Smoothie Recipe (R,V,GF)

Thanks for the recipe, Kathy!

(Recipe was adapted by Robyn.)

2 C spinach
1 C kale
7-8 strawberries
10-12 blueberries
2 packets stevia
1 Tbsp. milled flax seeds
1 C ice
8 oz. water

Put all in blender and blend well.

Peaches-and-Cream Green Smoothie (R,V,GF)

Thanks for the recipe, Kathy!

1 C almond milk (preferably unsweetened and homemade)
1 frozen banana, in chunks
1 tsp. vanilla extract
1 tsp. cinnamon
2-3 C spinach
1 C frozen peaches

Blend until smooth.

Pineapple-Cilantro Smoothie (R,V,GF)

Thanks for the recipe, Kelli!

1 bunch cilantro
½ small, fresh pineapple (including core)
2 fresh nectarines
1 C water
½ C ice
¼ tsp. almond extract

Blend all together and enjoy!

Avocado Dream (R,V,GF)

Thanks for the recipe, Kim!

6 oz. coconut liquid
2 hearty handfuls spinach
1 avocado
juice of ½ fresh lime
1 stevia packet

Blend coconut liquid and spinach till smooth. Then add the avocado, lime juice, and stevia and blend for 20 sec.

Chocó-Butter Smoothie (V,GF)

Thanks for the recipe, Kim!

2 C almond milk
1 Tbsp. raw cocoa
1 Tbsp. natural peanut butter
1 frozen banana
1-2 Tbsp. coconut oil

Add all ingredients to blender and blend. It makes a great mid-afternoon pick-me-up.

Not-Chocolate Smoothie (R,V)

Thanks for the recipe, Kirt!

4 C frozen banana chunks
almond milk or coconut milk, enough to almost cover the bananas
4 heaping spoonfuls raw or toasted carob
1 tsp. barley greens
1 Tbsp. raw cocoa nibs
1 Tbsp. chia seeds
optional: greens

Put bananas in blender, then add the milk to almost cover them. Then add rest of the ingredients. Blend until smooth

Grace's Favorite Fresh Smoothie (R,V,GF)

Thanks for the recipe, L Duba!

½ banana (fresh or frozen)
½ C frozen cherries (pitted) or mixed red berries
2-4 organic chard or collard leaves (or equivalent amount of organic lettuces)
stevia, to taste
16 oz. water (or more, as needed)
optional: 1 tsp. non-GMO stevia (can help replace banana as thickener)
optional: 1 bunch organic parsley

Put all ingredients into a blender and blend well.

Peachy Green Smoothie (R,V,GF)

Thanks for the recipe, Linda!

2 big handfuls fresh spinach
4 bananas (fresh or frozen)
2-3 C frozen peaches or nectarines
1 whole lemon, peeled
water, to desired consistency

Blend all in a high-powered blender and enjoy! The lemon adds just the right amount of fresh tartness!

Aspen's Awesome Almond Smoothie (GF)

Thanks for the recipe, Lisa (and Aspen, her 6-year-old daughter)!

3-4 C crushed ice
10 raw almonds
1 handful organic raspberries
2 C rice milk
1 C fresh or organic orange juice
3 Tbsp. Irish Cream (no alcohol and gluten-free)
1 C Greek yogurt with strawberries

Add all ingredients into a blender and blend to desired consistency. Top with a couple of extra almonds and serve!

Tip: We freeze organic raspberries when in season for use the rest of the year.

Refreshing Pear & Ginger Green Drink (R,V,GF)

Thanks for the recipe, Lisa Fielding (www.KISforhealth.com)!

1 lemon with half the peel removed
2 pears
1 C fresh pineapple
1" chunk fresh ginger
2 kale leaves
1 chard leaf (rainbow is best for vitamins)
2 handfuls spinach
water, to blend
stevia, to sweeten to taste

Blend on high until no more chunkies! Serve slightly chilled.

Whatever Green Smoothie (V,GF)

Thanks for the recipe, Lucia!

1 bunch kale
7 romaine lettuce leaves
2 Tbsp. coconut butter
1 pear, cored
½ banana
1 tsp. vanilla extract
½ C pure water
½ tsp. lecithin

Blend kale and lettuce in blender with water, coconut butter, vanilla, and lecithin. Add pear and banana and blend until smooth. (If you like it a little thinner, just add a little more water.)

Lynn's Garden of Eden (R,V,GF)

Thanks for the recipe, Lynn!

¼ C aloe vera juice
½ C almond milk
¼ C apple juice (organic, unsweetened)
¼ tsp. bluegreen algae
¼ tsp. barley
1 tsp. chia seeds
1 tsp. hemp hearts
1 Tbsp. freshly ground golden flax seeds
½ C frozen mango
½ C frozen pineapple
½ C frozen mixed berries
½ C fresh spinach
½ C fresh kale

Blend all ingredients in blender. If the mixture is too thick to blend, add a little more almond milk.

Caribbean Dream (R,V,GF)

Thanks for the recipe, Marci Hurd!

1 fresh mango
3 slices fresh pineapple
1 fresh kiwi
½ C fresh orange juice
1 C ice
2 handfuls spinach

Blend all and enjoy.

Favorite Smoothie (R,V,GF)

Thanks for the recipe, Marie-Lynn!

1 grapefruit (cut in half, squeeze juice into blender, and then scoop the rest of it in, including the seeds and pith)
2 servings stevia
2 bananas (3 if they're small)
2-3 handfuls raw spinach (or fill blender to the top)

Blend until desired consistency.

Hemp Smoothie (V,GF)

Thanks for the recipe, Marita!

¼ - ½ C unsweetened milk (rice, coconut, almond)
4 Tbsp. organic hemp protein
1 Tbsp. organic hemp seed oil
1 orange, cut into pieces

Blend all ingredients in blender until desired consistency.

Fresh Fruit Bowl (R,V,GF)

Thanks for the recipe, Marlene!

1 small organic red beet and its greens, washed
2 bananas
1 C blueberries
1 C strawberries
1 C mango
1 C pineapple
1 C fresh organic spinach
water and ice, to blend

Put all in blender and mix well.

Like Apple Pie (GF)

Thanks for the recipe, Marlys!

1 Fuji apple
2 celery stalks
1 handful spinach
1-2 Tbsp. coconut ghee
½ - ¾ C warm water (to melt the coconut ghee)
dash cinnamon
natural sweetener (your choice), to taste
splash vanilla
optional: 1 egg yolk, organic and free-range (it helps emulsify the coconut oil)

Blend all until smooth.

Grape-Banana Smoothie (R,V,GF)

Thanks for the recipe, Mary!

1 C grapes
1 banana
1-2 large handfuls spinach

Place all in blender and mix.

Morning Revival (R,V,GF)

Thanks for the recipe, Mary (Health Science Faculty at HCT - Fujairah Women's College)!

(Recipe was adapted by Robyn.)

¼ C beet juice
1 banana
¼ C sprouts
1 Tbsp. pomegranate seeds
few spinach leaves
2 romaine leaves
1 scoop green powder
¼ C almond, rice, or coconut milk
2 Tbsp. orange juice
6 ice cubes or frozen strawberries

Blend in a blender until smooth.

Silky Green pH Balancer (R,V,GF)

Thanks for the recipe, MaryAnn!

1 grapefruit, peeled and quartered
2 C spinach
2 kale leaves
1 cucumber
½ avocado
1 Tbsp. coconut oil
1 Tbsp. greens mix
½ -1 C water, as needed for desired consistency
optional: few drops stevia
optional: vanilla extract
optional: 2 Tbsp. raw hemp protein powder, if you want protein boost

Place all ingredients in blender and blend away!

Great-Tasting Green Shake (R,V,GF)

Thanks for the recipe, Max!

8" English cucumber
1 lime, peeled
1 whole avocado (meat only)
1 large handful baby spinach leaves
3 celery sticks
6-7 strawberries or raspberries
1 grapefruit (meat and juice only)
1 handful raisins
6-8 drops liquid stevia (NOW brand is ethanol-free extract)
1½ scoops Progressive VegeGreens Powder
1 Tbsp. almond butter [Use raw butter for R recipe.]
1 handful blueberries (when in season)
1 Tbsp. extra virgin coconut oil
5 ice cubes

Combine all ingredients and blend until creamy and smooth. *Makes 3-4 servings.*

Too-Good-To-Be-True Blueberry Smoothie (R,V,GF)

Thanks for the recipe, Melissa!

1 C frozen blueberries
1 ripe banana
1 C coconut milk
1 big handful spinach
touch of honey
optional: 1 scoop hemp powder

Add all ingredients to the blender and mix until at the desired consistency.

Breakfast Smoothie (V,GF)

Thanks for the recipe, Michelle!

1⅓ C organic, plain yogurt or kefir (homemade, if possible)
¾ ripe banana
3 frozen strawberries
¼ C blueberries
¼ C mixed berries
2 tsp. ground flax seeds
1 tsp. lemon-flavored fish oil
2 opened GABA capsules
2 opened acidophilus capsules (5 bill cells per capsule)
few drops Trace minerals
1 Tbsp. locally produced raw honey
optional: 1 scoop dehydrated greens *OR* 1 handful spinach

Blend on high and serve! Yummy!

Cinnamon-Banana Shake (R,V,GF)

Thanks for the recipe, Michelle!

1½ frozen bananas
8 oz. coconut water or coconut milk
½ tsp. cinnamon
1 packet stevia
2 C spinach
ice (if bananas aren't frozen)

Blend and serve. Yummy!

Yummy Micronutrient Green Smoothie (R,V,GF)

Thanks for the recipe, Mumtaz!

1-2 C micronutrient greens (any variety)
1-2 C pea sprouts
1 banana
½ orange
¼ pear
½ apple
½ large English cucumber
½" - 1" piece ginger
few sprigs coriander
optional: 1 C water or organic coconut water, if needed to thin out

Blend everything until smooth in a high-powered blender. If you feel it's too thick, add the water or coconut water. Enjoy.

Refreshing Mint Smoothie (R,V,GF)

Thanks for the recipe, Nanci!

1 cucumber
½ avocado
½ grapefruit
1 handful spinach
coconut water (to desired consistency)
ice cubes
mint leaves, to taste
stevia, to taste

Blend well.

Apple Pie Smoothie (R,V,GF)

Thanks for the recipe, Nancy!

1 C water
1 apple, cored
1 pear, cored
2 Medjool dates, pitted *OR* 1 persimmon
½ tsp. cinnamon
¼ tsp. ginger
2 frozen bananas, sliced
optional: use 2 peaches instead of the apple and pear

Blend all but the bananas, then add the bananas and blend again.

Berry-Swiss Chard Smoothie (R,V,GF)

Thanks for the recipe, Nancy!

1 C water
1 mango
1 banana
6 swiss chard leaves
1 C frozen raspberries
1-2 C frozen strawberries

Blend all but strawberries until smooth. Then while continuing to blend, add strawberries until desired thickness. *Makes 4 cups.*

Newbie Smoothie (V)

Thanks for the recipe, Nancy!

1 medium banana
1 C fresh pineapple
½ C coconut liquid or milk
4-5 kale leaves
3"-4" English cucumber (skin on—the flecks of dark green are pretty)
3 almonds (raw, soaked, skinned)
1 Tbsp. ground sesame seeds
1 Tbsp. ground flax seeds
½ C cooked basmati/bulgur mix

Add all to blender and mix until smooth. Enjoy!

Raspberry-Mango Cream (R,V,GF)

Thanks for the recipe, Nancy!

1 mango, cubed
1 C frozen raspberries
2 frozen bananas, sliced

Blend mango and raspberries in blender until smooth. Then blend in bananas. *Makes 3½ C.*

Mango Bango Green Smoothie (R,V,GF)

Thanks for the recipe, Natalie!

2-4 C fresh spinach
1-3 C water
2 oranges
2 frozen bananas
1 frozen mango

Add oranges, water, and spinach to the blender and blend until smooth. Then add remaining ingredients and blend until desired consistency (adding more water if necessary).

Green Deliciousness (R,V,GF)

Thanks for the recipe, Nicole!

2 C water

4 C spinach (or enough to blend in water to 4 C line on blender jar)

¼ C raw, organic agave

1 frozen banana

1 C frozen strawberries

Add all to blender and mix on high.

Lemon-Ginger Tonic Blast (R,V,GF)

Thanks for the recipe, Ondyena!

(Recipe was adapted by Robyn.)

To be taken every morning, to strengthen the immune system and alkalize the body. Perfect to drink a few times a day when you are ill. This tonic is anti-viral, anti-fungal, anti-bacterial, and a total-blood cleanser and tonic for the entire body. It makes your skin radiant and will get rid of dandruff or other skin problems. The lemon alkalizes the entire body.

1-2 apples

1-2 lemons (remove most of peel, leaving about 1" of the peel on one lemon)

huge chunk ginger (about 6")

¼ - 1 tsp. cayenne pepper (depending on heat units—use as much as you can tolerate)

1 large collard or kale leaf

1 Tbsp. cold-pressed coconut oil

Blend all ingredients with water (to your desired consistency) in high-powered blender, and optionally strain. [See Photos section.]

Reminds Me of Orange Julius (R,V,GF)

Thanks for the recipe, Pam!

(Recipe was adapted by Robyn.)

2 tangerines or clementines, peeled
1 C coconut or almond milk
¼ tsp. stevia powder
½ vanilla bean
8-9 ice cubes
1 Tbsp. flax seeds
optional: ½ C apple juice (organic, unsweetened)

Blend all in high-powered blender until smooth, about 90 sec.

Green Drink (R,V,GF)

Thanks for the recipe, Patty!

1 small can pineapple juice (no sugar added), chilled
1 celery stalk
½ cucumber, peeled
1 slice fresh ginger
1 large handful spinach

Blend in Blendtec and drink immediately. Yummy!

Spinach Green Smoothie (R,V,GF)

Thanks for the recipe, Patty!

2 handfuls spinach (or swiss chard or kale, for variety)
1 banana
1 apple
2 C water
2 scoops protein powder [Use vegan and/or raw powder for V and/or R recipe.]

Blend until all smooth. This is my favorite—but I also vary the fruit (works great with pineapple or blueberries too), but always use the banana.

Orange Bliss (R,V,GF)

Thanks for the recipe, Peggy!

1 orange
10 large frozen strawberries
2 C water
2 droppers full orange stevia
spring greens and spinach, to fill blender

Place first four ingredients in blender, then fill the remainder of the blender with spring greens and spinach. Blend to desired consistency and enjoy!

Zest Lady Green Smoothie (V,GF)

Thanks for the recipe, Peggy Carey, the Zest Lady (www.peggycarey.com/belean.html)!

1 C frozen papaya chunks
6 frozen strawberries
½ avocado
1 heaping tsp. carob powder
1 tsp. maca powder
1 scoop AIM Pro Peas vegetable protein
1 scoop AIM Fit n Fiber
2 tsp. AIM Leaf Greens live green powder
2 heaping tsp. AIM Barley Life Xtra
1 tsp. (or to taste) raw, organic agave
6-8 oz. water, depending on desired thickness

Blend until creamy.

PWS (Post-Workout Snack) (R,V,GF)

Thanks for the recipe, Pete!

4 bananas, divided
10 dried figs
¼ C goji berries
1 Tbsp. chia seeds

Soak the berries, figs, and seeds for a few minutes, and then blend with 2 bananas. Cut up other 2 bananas and pour mixture over them. Enjoy this nutritional powerhouse!

Green Avocado Smoothie (R,V,GF)

Thanks for the recipe, Peter!

½ ripe avocado
1 C spring water
4-5 dates *OR* ¼ tsp. stevia leaf powder
4 almonds
1 heaping tsp. Synergy Super Greens (spirulina, chlorella, barley grass, and wheat grass)

Blend all together very well.

Q's Strawberry Green Cream (R,V,GF)

Thanks for the recipe, Quinetta!

Because it is pretty creamy . . . .

1 clementine, peeled
6 strawberries with stems
½ avocado
¼ tsp. stevia liquid
2 Tbsp. ground flax seeds
3 large collard leaves
3 purple kale leaves
3-4 C spinach leaves
12 oz. water
optional: ½ C coconut kefir, strawberry flavor [Omit for raw recipe.]

Blend all very well until smooth and enjoy!

Orange Smoothie (R,V,GF)

Thanks for the recipe, Rebecca!

1 C water
½ fresh pineapple
½ fresh papaya
1 orange
1 lime
1 lb. frozen strawberries (approx.)
optional: ½ C goji berries

Put all ingredients except the strawberries in the blender and blend well. Fill any leftover space in the blender with the strawberries and blend again until smooth.

Purple Smoothie (R,V,GF)

Thanks for the recipe, Rick!

30 oz. water
2 Tbsp. pomegranate extract
1 handful frozen blueberries
1 handful black cherries
1 banana
few handfuls spinach and/or kale
2 celery stalks

Combine all ingredients in blender and blend until smooth.

Rita's Favorite Green Smoothie (R,V,GF)

Thanks for the recipe, Rita!

1 lb. spinach
1 bunch cilantro
½ lemon, unpeeled and cut into small cubes
½ grapefruit, peeled and cut into small cubes
½ orange, peeled and cut into small cubes
1 C frozen blueberries
3 frozen bananas
4 Tbsp. chia seeds
4 Tbsp. hemp seeds
4 C filtered water
green stevia powder, to taste

Place chia and hemp seeds in high-powered blender and grind to a powder, stirring if needed, and then grind again. Add water, all citrus cubes, blueberries, and bananas, then blend again. Add all greens and blend again. Top off with water if needed for desired consistency, then blend one more time.

Rita's Green Kick (R,V,GF)

Thanks for the recipe, Rita!

1 carton coconut water
1 large Granny Smith apple
1 fistful organic cilantro
½ small organic lime, with peel
2 small slices fresh ginger

Blend in blender until smooth.

Flexible Green Smoothie (R,V,GF)

Thanks for the recipe, Russ!

3 celery stalks
6" cucumber
2" raw ginger
½" hot pepper (more or less, depending how hot the pepper is and your tolerance)
1 avocado
1 papaya
spinach or other greens, to fill to top of blender
8 oz. water or fresh-squeezed fruit juice
optional: favorite fruits and/or super foods, as desired

Put first six ingredients into the blender, then fill to the top with greens. Add water or fruit juice. Blend until well mixed. Add optional fruits and super foods, then blend again.

Pecan Apple Smoothie Leather (R,V,GF)

Thanks for the recipe, Sandra!

3 apples
½ C pecans
½ C flax seeds
10 dates

Blend the pecans and flax seeds. Separately purée the apples, then mix with the dates. Combine with the pecans and flaxseed mixture and dehydrate until soft or crisp, as desired.

Best Breakfast Smoothie (R,V,GF)

Thanks for the recipe, Sarah!

1 C water
1 banana
1 pear
1 apple
1 handful kale leaves, stems removed *OR* 1 big handful baby spinach (can also use cilantro or parsley)
1 celery stalk

Blend in blender until desired consistency. Not too sweet, not too green!

Berry Blast (R,V,GF)

Thanks for the recipe, Sean!

2 C spinach
2 oranges, peeled (leave the white on the oranges for riboflavin)
½ C frozen strawberries*
½ C frozen blueberries*
½ C frozen raspberries*
filtered water (to desired thickness)

**Can substitute fresh berries and ice.*

Blend all in high-powered blender until smooth.

Greena Colada (R,V,GF)

Thanks for the recipe, Sean!

2 C spinach
2 C unsweetened vanilla almond milk or coconut milk [Use homemade milk for R recipe.]
1 C raw coconut (dried or young fresh)
1½ C frozen pineapple *OR* 1 C fresh pineapple + 2 C ice cubes
filtered water, to desired thickness

Blend all in blender until smooth. [See Photos section.]

Blushing Bunny (R,V,GF)

Thanks for the recipe, Sharli!

1 C carrot juice
1 C almond milk
8-12 strawberries
1 banana
optional: kale or spinach

Blend all until smooth. It is particularly yummy if the bananas or the strawberries are frozen. [See Photos section.]

Sharon's Special (R,V,GF)

Thanks for the recipe, Sharon in Australia!

1 C spring water
1 handful raw almonds (or any other mixed seeds and nuts)
8 dried apricots
½ C mixed dried fruit of your choice (figs, prunes, sultanas, dates)
fresh coconut meat/flakes, to taste
1-2 apples or pears (you can also use nashis/Asian pears, peaches, nectarines, a few big slices of pineapple, a mango, or 1-2 bananas depending on their size and how many people it is for)
1 tsp. organic spirulina powder per person
optional: 1 Tbsp. tahini
optional: 1 Tbsp. unsweetened yogurt [Omit for raw and vegan recipe.]
optional: 2 tsp. flaxseed oil

In blender pitcher, soak almonds, dried apricots, and dried fruit mix overnight in spring water. In the morning, blend the soaked mixture. Then add the rest of the ingredients and blend again, adding a bit more spring water to make it the consistency you desire. Yum!

Note: It is nice to have the different fruits on different days to change the flavor and texture each day!

Coconut-Citrus Green Divine Smoothie (V,GF)

Thanks for the recipe, Shirly (holistic health counselor & conscious living coach)!

1 C light coconut milk
½ large cucumber
juice of 1 large lemon
1 small-to-medium orange or tangerine, peeled
2-3 C organic greens (like spinach or salad blends)
1 heaping tsp. green powder
5 ice cubes (approx.)
sweetener, to taste

Add all ingredients into blender and blend. Refreshing and delicious.

Fruity Green Cacao (V,GF)

Thanks for the recipe, Shirly (holistic health counselor & conscious living coach)!

An ultra-satisfying way to begin your day!

1 C light coconut milk
1 organic banana
½ - 1 C frozen organic blueberries
½ - 1 C water
1 scoop your favorite green powder (I like Vitamineral Green or Dragon Herb's Tonic Alchemy)
1 heaping Tbsp. raw cacao (I like Sunfire Foods Cacao or Essential Living Foods)
1 tsp. mesquite
2-3 C organic fresh greens (I like to mix spinach and baby romaine mixes)
sweetener, to taste
optional: pinch Original Crystal Himalayan Salt

Put all ingredients into a blender and mix well.

Mommy's "Monster Blood" Smoothie (V,GF)

Thanks for the recipe, Stacey!

2 handfuls organic spinach
1-1½ C water
1 ripe avocado
1 kiwi fruit
½ banana
½ C frozen mixed berries (any kind)
2 Tbsp. coconut powder
2 Tbsp. ground flax seeds
optional: 1 scoop your favorite protein powder *OR* 2 Tbsp. kefir/yogurt

Add all to blender and blend until smooth.

Tropical Nut Smoothie (GF)

Thanks for the recipe, Stacey!

1 can coconut milk
16 oz. pineapple, mango, or passion fruit (fresh or frozen)
4 oz. plain yogurt
8 oz. apple juice (organic, unsweetened)
ice cubes
½ tsp. nutmeg
1 boost (a vitamin, protein powder, spinach, etc., of your choice)

Combine all ingredients into blender and mix well. Enjoy!

Fruit & Vegetable Smoothie (GF)

Thanks for the recipe, Stephen!

12 oz. water
2 handfuls spinach
1 carrot
1 small handful snow peas
1 small handful green beans
2 Tbsp. vanilla yogurt
½ avocado
½ banana
2 scoops ground flax seeds
2 scoops vanilla rice protein
¼ lemon

Blend water, spinach, carrot, peas and beans. Then add the remaining ingredients and blend until smooth.

Berry Green Smoothie (R,V,GF)

Thanks for the recipe, SZQ in Alaska

(Recipe was adapted by Robyn.)

It mixes up a nice, deep red color and appeals to even the greatest skeptics in my life!

1 orange
2-3 handfuls greens
1 small-medium (or ½ large) banana
1-2 C (about 12) frozen strawberries
½ C frozen raspberries

Blend all ingredients in blender until desired consistency.

Note: Variations on the theme may include substituting 3-4 frozen wheat grass cubes for the greens, another fresh fruit for the banana (I love fresh mango), and different frozen fruits (although I keep it mostly berries).

Pear-y Kale Smoothie (R,V,GF)

Thanks for the recipe, Teresa!

(Recipe was adapted by Robyn.)

1 C green grapes
1 orange, peeled
1 frozen banana
1 pear, cored
2 kale leaves, including stems
½ C water, or more to desired consistency
2 C ice cubes

Mix on high in blender until smooth. *Makes 1 serving.*

Montel Williams' Green Smoothie (R,V,GF)

Thanks for the recipe, Teresa!

2 frozen bananas, in chunks
3 oranges
1 head romaine lettuce
2 C cold water
2 C ice

Blend well in a high-powered blender. *Serves 2-3.*

Cocoa Berry Protein Smoothie Shake (V,GF)

Thanks for the recipe, Terry in Brentwood, CA!

1 C frozen strawberries (or any frozen berries or fruit of your choice), organic and unsweetened
12 oz. water (approx.)
1 serving Coco Pure
1 tsp. cocoa powder (over 72%), non-alkalized and organic
stevia, to taste (to make it super-chocolaty, use Nu Naturals chocolate stevia)
3-4 ice cubes
optional: 1 serving high-quality protein powder and more water as needed
optional: 1 tsp. ground flax seeds
optional: 1 tsp. flaxseed or coconut oil

Place all in blender and blend well. Makes a nice, thick, super-chocolaty shake. Yummy!

Tiffany's Spinach Smoothie (R,V,GF)

Thanks for the recipe, Tiffany!

2-3 handfuls spinach
1 mango
2 peaches
protein powder (I like to use hemp or hemp seeds)
apple juice (organic, unsweetened), as needed for desired consistency

Blend all in blender. I use all organic ingredients and also juice my own apples when possible. Enjoy!

Hopper's Favorite Smoothie (R,V,GF)

Thanks for the recipe, Vicky!

flax seeds
2 carrots
1 large handful spinach
½ avocado
1 lemon
1 handful strawberries
½ cucumber
3 kale leaves
1 packet Truvia
1 collard greens leaf
20 oz ionized water
1 handful sprouted almonds

Add all ingredients to blender and mix until smooth.

Anon Smoothie (R,V,GF)

Thanks for the recipe, Vikki!

This is an adaptation of one of Victoria Boutenko's recipes.

2 apples
1 bunch parsley
greens mixture (spinach, bok choi, kale, spring greens)
1 C water
½ C ice
¼ lemon (with rind)

Blend all until very smooth in a high-powered blender.

Other Drinks

Winter Wassail (R,V,GF)

Thanks for the recipe, Jenna!

4 qt. apple juice or apple cider*
2 C fresh orange juice*
1 C fresh lemon juice*
1 C fresh pineapple juice*
1 stick whole cinnamon
1 tsp. whole cloves (placed in a tea ball or cheesecloth bag, if desired)

**If not using fresh juices, be sure they are unsweetened.*

Combine all ingredients in large pot. Cover and bring to a simmer. Make sure to keep below 115° if using raw/fresh juices. Strain, if cloves are loose. Serve warm.

Tip: Serves well from a Crockpot. If serving at a party, slices of oranges and lemons floating in the wassail are pretty. I like this just as well served cold. I'll put the leftovers in a pitcher and usually put the cinnamon stick in there too. Stays yummy in the fridge for several days.

Hot Chocolate (R,V,GF)

Thanks for the recipe, Judy!

Note: This recipe is raw only if you don't heat it over 115°!

1 tsp. raw cocoa powder
1 Tbsp. agave nectar
dash vanilla
1 C milk (coconut, almond, rice)

Mix all in a saucepan on the stove and warm to desired temperature. *Makes 1 C.* [See Photos section.]